MISSING

Without a Trace

8 Days of Horror

PALM BEACH COUNTY
LIBRARY SYSTEM
3650 Summit Boulevard
West Palm Beach, FL 33406-4198

MISSING

Without a Trace

8 Days of Horror

Tanya Rider and Tracy C. Ertl
with Carol Lieberman, M.D.

TitleTown
PUBLISHING

Missing Without a Trace: *8 Days of Horror*

TitleTown Publishing, LLC
P.O. Box 12093 Green Bay, WI 54307-12093
920.737.8051 | titletownpublishing.com

Edited by Katie Vecchio
Cover design by Erika L. Block
Interior layout and design by Erika L. Block

PUBLISHER'S CATALOGING-IN-PUBLICATION DATA:

Rider, Tanya.
Missing Without a Trace : 8 days of horror / Tanya Rider and Tracy C.
Ertl. -- 1st ed. -- Green Bay, WI : TitleTown Pub., c2011.
p. ; cm.
ISBN: 978-0-9823008-6-2
1. Rider, Tanya. 2. Adult child abuse victims--Psychological
aspects. 3. Traffic accident victims--Psychological aspects.
4. Survival after airplane accidents, shipwrecks, etc. 5. Missing
persons--Investigation--Washington (State)--King County.
6. Missing persons--Investigation--United States--States. I. Ertl,
Tracy C. II. Title.
HV6762.U6 R53 2011
363.2/336--dc22 1101

Printed in the USA by Thomson-Shore
first edition ♻ printed on recycled paper
10 9 8 7 6 5 4 3 2 1

CONTENTS

ACKNOWLEDGMENTS

Missing Without a Trace would not have been possible without the continual support of my family. My children—Andrew, Christine and Bradley—believed in the importance of *Missing* from the beginning. Bradley accompanied me to Rock Island where I wrote part of the manuscript. He, along with my brother, Stephen, provided sanctuary in the evenings when I desperately needed to relax and debrief from intense writing sessions.

My publicist, Michael Wright, who is vice president of Garson & Wright Public Relations, was the guiding force behind this project. Without him, there would be no *Missing Without a Trace*. Wright gave his vision for the book and infused his energy at times when we felt we had nothing left to give to the partnership. I will always be deeply grateful to him for believing in TitleTown's ability to produce the book and in me to write it with proper care for the heart of a survivor.

The TitleTown team was invincible. Katie Vecchio not only edited *Missing* but also stepped in as a significant ghost voice when my publishing responsibilities swallowed additional writing time. Designer Erika Block captured the essence of a missing person with an undeniably brilliant cover and interior design. Both Block and Vecchio worked long, grueling hours. Research assistants Jessica Engman and Katie Stilp were invaluable in gathering extensive information on the missing person process. Without their expertise, the book would be incomplete.

Brown County Public Safety Communications, a multi-jurisdiction emergency-response center handling fire, police and EMS calls in Green Bay, Wisconsin, is my second family and has provided me with a backdrop of understanding and passion for survival topics unprecedented by any publisher in the industry today. My 911 family has waited in anticipation of this title as they know writing and publishing has always been my other love and my destiny.

I thank my friends for accepting my absence while I was trying to bring voice to Tanya Rider and the plight of other survivors like her.

My associates at the Association for Public Safety Communications Officials (APCO) have been supportive in my chase of this project and brought me in direct connection with the NCMEC staff, who give their lives to the missing and those who are searching for them.

I extend my deep gratitude to the men and women of law enforcement who dedicate themselves to the pursuit of the lost, taken and missing. We need you.

I thank Dr. Carole Lieberman, who accompanied me to Seattle, Washington, to work with Tanya Rider in the hopes of bringing greater understanding to the process of being a survivor. There is no timeline to healing and we must be patient in its pursuit. That, perhaps, is the greatest lesson in *Missing*.

Lastly, I thank Tanya Rider for trusting me to help her tell her unbelievable story of survival against every odd. Tanya, you are a true survivor and it is my honor to have learned your story and been given the chance to share it with others, both as your co-author and publisher. God bless you.

—Tracy C. Ertl

Acknowledgments

No matter what, my husband Tom is the one person in the world who has always been there for me—and always will be—and I want to thank him for so much. He can be a pain but he is *my* pain, and I thank him for never giving up on me! To help him get through his anger, he wrote for therapy, and he has shown me how to vent constructively. It was Tom's idea to write about my story and our situation.

I'd like to thank many people in the public for your love, concern and prayers for my recovery as well as for your cards and letters of encouragement. I extend a special "Thank you!" to the person who went down into that hole that was my home for eight days to bring me my books and papers. You were very kind and considerate to do this and I will never forget your thoughtful, anonymous act. I'll always be thankful.

So many people stepped up to help in any way they could and I am so grateful to all of them. I thank several nurses, doctors and other caregivers who went above and beyond to save my leg. I even want to thank the nurse who threatened me with a nursing home! More than anyone else, she motivated me to get home and convinced me that I could not live under the control of other people!

Most of all, I thank God. If not for my faith in Him, I don't know where I would be now. Without His help, I could never have survived for eight days. Without His protection from the pure horror, I would probably be insane and lost to the world. Without His love, I would probably not have had the strength to cope with my injuries. I thank God for keeping me alive and, for the most part, whole.

—*Tanya Rider*

First, I want to thank my wife, Tanya. Thanks to her pure spirit and iron will—and through the grace of God—Tanya fought her way back from death's door. Through everything that she had to endure, her courage never wavered. She fought to keep her leg as well as her life, and has had to live through many trials that would have destroyed a lesser person. I know that, if I had been trapped in that ravine, I probably would have been dead long before they found me, and I am *so* grateful that Tanya returned to me.

While she survived for eight days without food or water, her body began the process of shutting down; her cells diverted the precious fluid that pumped through her veins, began to consume her muscles to produce energy, and damaged her kidneys. By the time she was finally found, Tanya was well past the point of any rational hope for survival.

My employer at the time—Gary Racca, owner of SoundBuilt Homes—did so many things to support us and to make our lives easier in those first few weeks after Tanya was rescued. I would never have asked anyone in the world for the things that Gary and my coworkers at SoundBuilt did for us, and they did it all without my asking—even offered up their vacation days to help cook or clean for Tanya when she got home. Throughout the ordeal, they were the best people I could have had around me when I needed them the most. I thank all of them from the bottom of my heart.

I also want to offer a heartfelt thanks to my friend Adam, who took care of our dog for those first few weeks, allowing me to stay at the hospital with Tanya full time. And words can never express my gratitude to all of the people who pitched in to make life a little easier for Tanya and me.

Through Tanya's recovery, no matter how many times her doctors cautioned her not to get too optimistic, she displayed incomparable drive and absolute determination to get herself out of the hospital. Her strong will and refusal to quit fueled her daily routine for months on end and stunned all of her treating doctors and everyone who heard her story. Later, this same drive motivated her to return to work, which provided us with health insurance; this is how Tanya saved my life, as I was soon diagnosed with dangerous diabetes.

Battling infection after infection, Tanya continues to work hard. With every two steps forward, she hits another bump in the road, and I sometimes worry that she will reach a point when she does not want to fight anymore. But, with every bump, she gets back up and takes the next two steps. And though the road ahead is marred with more battles, Tanya fights on. As she does, part of me knows that she fights for me because she knows I need her. Though I am filled with pride, it is tainted with sorrow. Watching firsthand as she fights so many battles, I wish that she didn't have to fight. I wish that she could have it easy for a while and be able to have some fun.

For now, I believe that God's plans for her are much greater than I can now know. But I do know that my beautiful wife Tanya is the strongest woman I know. She is my hero. I pray that the future brings her all that she could ever want, and that she wins her fight sooner rather than later.

—Tom Rider

PREFACE

My heart pounded. I tried to slow my breathing, to control the fear crawling through my mind. I wanted to focus on the computer screen but I felt panicky. My stomach swirled with nausea as I realized that one wrong move would send me tumbling off the rock ledge that barely held my body and my laptop.

I put myself on the precarious but gorgeous ledge seventy feet above the rocks and water of the coast of Rock Island in Door County, Wisconsin. Entrusted to write Tanya Rider's survival story, I wanted to try to put myself in her place—a place of terror and desperation—so that I could capture her respirations, her sense of imprisonment and the cramped feeling of being unable to move and held against her will.

Curled up there and trying to write, I drank water. I continued to drink, even when I felt like I had to go to the bathroom. I wanted to feel the intense pain of needing to use the restroom—and trying desperately not to void on myself. A 911 dispatcher for eighteen years, I have had to stay locked in place for hours while on the phone with a suicidal caller or while dispatching during a weapon call. Forgoing a bathroom break is one of the requirements of the profession.

When I was a young girl, my father would load all of us into the car for a road trip and use bathroom stops to control us. However, I had never been forced to make the decision to soil myself and sit in it. There is something subhuman about that process. But, over and over again and for more than a week, Tanya Rider was forced to surrender that control of her body while she was trapped in her car. I could not ghost her story without moving through some of that pain, humiliation, filth and acceptance of predicament.

The ledge on Rock Island became my captor as I wrote much of *Missing Without a Trace*. I wanted to feel the claustrophobia and inability to breathe that must have come when Tanya realized that her legs were pinned, she was harnessed in, no one could hear her and no one was coming. As a reader, you will probably be able to feel through the writing when I hit the most difficult moments.

Although I had free will to leave, I pinned my body up against a sheet of rock in a small, open cave on the island and, again, I wrote on my laptop, trying to bring you into Tanya Rider's SUV as she fought to hang on.

As you will learn from Tanya's story, she feels blessed to be alive and to have emerged from the missing, and she thanks God for giving her the strength to make it. She is one of the lucky ones, who made it home. Tanya is a survivor, but not a writer. She wanted to be able to share her story with others so that they might know the power of faith. She also hopes for changes in law enforcement protocols for the handling of missing person reports.

Tanya Rider came to me uniquely. Apprised of my work as a publisher, Tanya knew nothing of my background as a dispatcher and national instructor in missing persons protocol. A 911 dispatcher for almost two decades, I have heard the cries of parents and loved ones when they called in to report their family members missing, and I have been on the receiving end of the joyful calls, when loved ones have returned or when we somehow reunited them. I am also a volunteer instructor for the National Center for Missing and Exploited Children (and Adults), and I teach protocol on how to increase the odds of finding our missing across the country.

Because Tanya was left in the ravine without a proper search, I viewed her as a victim who suffered an unbelievable ordeal of pain and trauma. But most of our missing never come home, and so I also viewed Tanya as an incredibly lucky survivor. Although her journey begins with a terrible accident, her story is more about survival and missing persons than anything else.

It is a risk to try to partially ghost write the very book that I have agreed to publish, but Tanya's story commanded my passion for the subject to such a degree that I was simply unwilling to give her to someone else. Since nearly everyone else seemed to have failed Tanya, I wanted to ensure a proper journey with her story. The endeavor was daunting and I brought in another ghost to help.

Writing *Missing Without a Trace* was painful. As a 911 professional, I am very much a part of the family of law enforcement and the centers that support them. Punished within the media for the slightest error and judged by a public that rarely understands our processes or constraints, those of us in law enforcement are taught never to sit in judgment of our own. However, some of the material in this book exposes mistakes made by my second family—the law enforcement community. Though this was hard for me to write and publish, humbly I believe that we *must* examine what we have done so that we can have a chance to improve our service to the missing and the families who are looking for them.

My own agency, Brown County Public Safety Communications, is currently working in unison with the law enforcement agencies we serve to create a missing person protocol that safeguards the public while diligently using our limited resources. NCMEC has combined forces with several federal and private agencies to form best-practice standards in handling the missing. As a proponent of standards, I hope that we can avoid anyone else suffering the near death experience and subsequent trauma that Tanya Rider has endured.

In March 2009, I went to NCMEC headquarters in Alexandria, Virginia, to attend an executive training program for law enforcement professionals and policy implementers. NCMEC taught us the best case protocol and practices when working with missing person and exploitation cases. One of our victim/survivor speakers was Colleen Nick, founder of the Morgan Nick Foundation. While I had always had an interest in writing or publishing stories about the plight of the missing, Colleen Nick was the person who gave me the courage to take Tanya Rider's story and to give voice to her experience.

Colleen recounted to us the story of her abducted six-year-old daughter, Morgan. In 1995, Colleen and other parents were sitting in the simple stands of a small town Arkansas baseball field, cheering the children who played ball on the diamond. Just a few feet away, in the adjoining dirt parking lot, Morgan and some other children chased fireflies and giggled with joy, as children do. Minutes later, when the game ended, the parking lot cleared. Morgan was missing.

The last image of Morgan was of her smiling while she removed one of her shoes and dumped the sand out of it. She bent down, presumably to put her shoe back on, and no one reported seeing her again. Ever. Witnesses recounted seeing an unknown male in a red truck.

Listening to Colleen, we sat motionless in the room. It was the first time in years I had seen silent tears from police chiefs and other administrators, assembled from all over the country and hoping to make a difference in the lives of missing children, missing adults and their families.

Colleen Nick cried openly but with full grace as she described the journey of her search for Morgan over the years that would follow.

We all stopped breathing again when Colleen asserted, at the end of her speech, that though it was 1995 when Morgan disappeared, she still believed that Morgan was out there. Morgan needs to be brought home, said Colleen, who has not given up the search because "a mother knows." *All* of our missing, she said, deserve to have that search.

She is right, and I am with her. Just months after that training program, this belief was renewed once again with the astounding recovery of Jaycee Dugard, who was kidnapped at age eleven and recovered at age twenty-eight.

Regardless of circumstance or odds, *every* missing person deserves to be searched for, and we—American law enforcement—need to follow up, to search, to investigate, and to bring to bear any and all available resources and technology.

One problem is that we must balance this imperative with the rights of people who *want* to go missing, to start a new life or to escape those who have harmed them in the past. *Missing Without a Trace* explores these issues. In the process, we hope to create discussion and bring changes and improvements in these areas.

Though you will likely feel much anger through the book, *Missing* is not a witch hunt. It was impossible to capture the story of Tanya Rider and leave out the anger she felt while left to rot in the ravine. Trying to put their lives back together, Tanya and her husband have also experienced much helplessness and hopelessness in the years after the accident. Still, they press on, and Tanya continues to express incredible faith in God to move her and her family on to a better place.

More important than anger is that *any* of us could become one of the missing at any time. *Any of us* could say goodbye to our sweetheart or our child and have them disappear without a trace. If you knew in advance that *you* were going to go missing sometime in the next forty-eight hours, or you knew that someone you couldn't live without was about to go missing, what would you do to prepare? What *could* you do? We wrote *Missing*

Without a Trace to prepare you and those you love for the unthinkable, because you *can* increase your odds of surviving and making your way back to your family, and you *can* increase the odds of getting your child back. *Missing* provides concrete suggestions to help you and your loved ones remain safe—and to know what to do when you aren't.

By watching the success of people who have navigated trauma and adversity, we learn to handle it ourselves. Though Tanya Rider remains in much pain today—and she faces many challenges—she is a survivor. Conducting the research for this book, my team and I contacted many professionals who called Tanya a miracle. I think she *is* a miracle, but there were physical and psychological components that helped her make it to that eighth day. I believe anyone can learn from her, take that information and apply it to their own challenges and traumas. Thus, I have designed *Missing* to provide you with practical information to help you and your loved ones to survive tragedy, and also to help you believe again in the miracle of the impossible through the eyes of an indomitable survivor.

—Tracy C. Ertl

PROLOGUE

Trapped—Again

By Carole Lieberman, M.D.

When Tanya Rider's SUV, which she'd fondly named Skywalker, went over the embankment on a rural road outside of Seattle, it ruthlessly trapped her inside. But the feeling of being held prisoner in a nightmarish world that she could not control was all-too familiar to her. The cold metal carcass that entombed her in the ravine by the side of the road replicated the walls of the cold loveless homes that had entombed her as a child. And just as no one 'saw' her or felt her pain when she was a little girl, because they were too self-absorbed to look, no one 'saw' her this time, either, despite the missing-person reports and the countless cars that passed as the hours ticked by. Indeed, she was trapped—again.

Tanya's mother, Nancy, was very young when she met Randy, the man who would become Tanya's father. Though her parents had picked up on warning signs that Nancy had missed, she married him anyway, despite their disapproval. Randy's good looks and charm fleetingly concealed his dark side: drug addiction and a violent temper. Tanya was born in 1974, when Nancy was nineteen and Randy was twenty-one. As it turned out, when Tanya was a baby, he beat Nancy and their tumultuous marriage ended. Tanya's grandmother quietly planned to move Nancy and Tanya across the country. The night before they left, Randy got wind of this. He stole the furniture that the grandmother had provided, as well as Tanya's baby clothes and toys. According to Tanya, Randy's problems with drugs then drove him to break into a pharmacy to feed his habit, and landed him in a federal penitentiary. The next time she saw her father, Tanya was entering adolescence. She had not been given a choice to see him sooner and she had desperately longed for him.

Living with her mom was like living in a house of horrors. Nancy, lonely and miserable, turned to different men and nightly parties, where drugs and alcohol were served. Sometimes, Nancy hosted these parties at home. Other times, she went to the men's homes and taught Tanya, at a young age, to make sure to lock the door while she was left home alone.

There was never adequate food in the house. "My whole childhood was about starvation," she recalls. Growing up, her diet consisted of Froot Loops, Pop-Tarts, chili and rice. When Tanya's grandmother gave her money for doing chores, Tanya used it to buy food. If her mother cooked, which was rare, it was because Nancy's latest boyfriend was there. "My mother gave me dirty looks if I came out when her boyfriend was there, or when she was having a party," Tanya says. "So I spent lots of time in my room with my Barbies."

Nancy continued choosing 'bad boy' types who beat her, just as Randy had done. One man, who was her boyfriend for eight years, was repeatedly abusive. At times, Nancy and Tanya had to flee from him in the middle of the night. Tanya recalls being in the car, alone in the dark, while her mother knocked on doors, asking people if they would let her use their phone to call the police. Then, Tanya and her mother would sit in the car, waiting for the police to come and arrest the boyfriend. As he was being handcuffed, he screamed, "Tanya, don't let them take me away!" Each time, he'd leave for a while, but then he'd come back. Tanya tried to tell her mother that these men weren't good for her, but her mother didn't listen.

To soothe herself, throughout her childhood, Tanya would dream of her father. She'd tell herself, "I bet I have the greatest dad out there. He's gonna find me one day and take me away!" The first discussion Tanya remembers about her dad threatened to smash these dreams, when she was six years old. Nancy and her boyfriend (the one who lasted eight years) were in bed. Tanya had a nightmare and came running to her mom for comfort. Nancy's boyfriend, apparently annoyed that Tanya was disturbing them, told her that her father was in prison because he's a very bad man. Still, to get through the real-life nightmare of her childhood, Tanya held on to her dreams of her dad, believing that he would rescue her one day.

When she wasn't neglecting Tanya, Nancy was pulling her hair, kicking her, throwing her against a wall, and beating her with a belt. Her mother told her not to cry, or it would make it worse. Tanya looked a lot like her father, and this triggered her mother's feelings of rejection and anger towards him, which Nancy displaced onto Tanya. "I blocked out a lot of it," a downcast Tanya explains.

As a child, Tanya also dreamed that someone took away her mother, because she couldn't understand how her mother could be so many different personalities. If Tanya had a cold, Nancy was nurturing. But, other times, Nancy, herself, was still a little girl who would not grow up. She was dependent on others, including Tanya. Yet, with her boyfriends, Nancy was all about make-up and being sexy. This was all very confusing to little Tanya.

Elementary school was tough. Tanya recalls that she was always picked on because she was an easy target, from her clothes to her obvious insecurities. She was jabbed in the leg with a pencil in class and kicked at the bus stop. Tanya, being the victim of abuse at home, invited kids to abuse her, as if she were wearing a sign.

Junior high was no better. Tanya continued to be picked on but, now, in more insidious ways. For example, someone once passed her a note, pretending to be a popular guy asking her out on a date. She went up to him after class and he laughed at her because he hadn't sent the note.

When Tanya was young, her maternal grandparents were loving substitute parents. But, they traveled a lot and she could not rely upon them to rescue her from all the neglect and abuse. The weekends she was able to be with them, they treated Tanya like a princess, making her breakfast and spoiling her with lots of Barbie dolls and other indulgences. But this only further infuriated Nancy, who was jealous of all their pampering.

Tanya's mother had warned her not to tell her grandparents about Nancy's boyfriends and her partying, threatening to beat Tanya if she dared speak of it. Finally, when Tanya was twelve or thirteen, unable to withstand it any longer, she told her grandparents about her mother's abuse. Her grandfather swiftly took her home so that Tanya could show him the belt her mom used, and then took her to Child Protective Services. They ordered Tanya and her mom into counseling. This prompted Nancy to call Randy, who had gotten out of prison, built a painting business and remarried. Nancy was in trouble, so she decided it was time to bring him back into the picture.

Nancy called Randy, inquiring—out of the blue—if he would like to have Tanya come live with them. This seemed like a wonderful idea to Tanya. She had visions of a real family, a comfortable home, dinners… a normal life. "I could be a kid," she thought. So she decided to live with her dad. And she did, for one-and-a-half-years, from twelve or thirteen years old until she was fourteen or fifteen.

But whereas living with her mom meant complete neglect, living with her dad meant every move she made was wrong. Although her father spoiled her with expensive things from the mall, her perfectionist stepmother treated Tanya like Cinderella, making her clean house and do chores. She was very afraid of them. When Tanya accidentally broke something while she was cleaning, her father's face got beet red and he yelled at her that she was "slime." Another time, he threw down a chair and threatened to cut off her long hair, which he did, ostensibly because her hair products were costing him too much money. It was another way to show her that he was in control. His displeasure and yelling was a frequent occurrence.

Tanya's stepmother couldn't have children. She was afraid that Tanya would take her father with her when she returned to Washington, and that he would return to his first love, Nancy. So her stepmother never missed an opportunity to complain to him about Tanya. She read Tanya's diary and eavesdropped outside her therapy sessions, exposing Tanya's most personal thoughts, such as the reason why she refused to call Randy "Dad"—because he was never around during her childhood.

Since Randy's brother had starved himself to death, Tanya wasn't allowed to close her door. As a teenage girl, she found this very awkward and uncomfortable. She was even told how long she could be in the shower. Tanya tried her best. She was a straight-A student, but this wasn't enough for them. She had to be in honor classes. The social worker from Child Protective Services was still in contact with her, but Tanya couldn't tell her how things really were at her dad's house because her calls were being monitored.

Still, this was a time when Tanya began to flourish. Now in eighth and ninth grade, she became a top student and others looked up to her. She played violin and was involved in the drama group. But her overprotective father and stepmother interfered, restricting her from acting in the school play and from going on a school trip to see the space shuttle.

After a year and a half, it was agreed upon that she would visit her mother for summer vacation. Her father was afraid she'd stay there, so he wouldn't let her take her clothes with her when she left. When Tanya got home to Washington, her mother was being very sweet, and this contrasted with the strict rules she'd been made to obey at her dad's. Her mom convinced her to stay longer. But, when her father heard this, he told Tanya in no uncertain terms that she could either come back right then or not at all! She chose the latter.

It was the summer before tenth grade. At first, life with mom was better than before. Nancy had gotten a steady job as a Boeing secretary, as well as a settlement from a car accident, so they were able to move from low-rent subsidized housing into a better apartment near the high school that Tanya wanted to attend. In high school, Tanya was an honor student, belonged to the Honor Society and Future Business Leaders of America, and had friends.

But her mom was still gone every night, coming back in the morning to get ready for work. Nancy didn't bring guys home anymore, now that Tanya had blossomed into a beautiful teenager. She was jealous of her daughter and didn't want to have to compete with her. Sometimes, Nancy would be incoherent and, soon, she became abusive again. She bit Tanya and threw things at her. This time, Tanya let people know. Sometimes she stayed with friends. Once, when Tanya ran away, her friend's mother called the police to report the abuse. Tanya became depressed. She started missing school and losing friends, who told her she was dragging them down.

During the tenth grade and into the first half of eleventh grade, Tanya had a boyfriend named Steven. They were never intimate, but dated a lot in groups and had fun. Then, one day, a girl who had a crush on Steven played a nasty trick on Tanya, hoping that it would make them break up. She told Tanya that another boy, on whom Tanya had a secret crush, wanted to go out with her. She goaded Tanya into calling him and essentially asking him out. They went on only one date because he was pining after some other girl and wasn't into Tanya. When Steven found out, he was devastated. He dumped Tanya and wouldn't even talk to her. This is when Tanya's severe depression truly set in.

Sometime during her junior year, her grandparents thought it would be best if Tanya came to live with them for a year, from approximately age sixteen to seventeen. This meant she had to transfer to a different high school, which she recalls as an unhappy place. Steven visited her at her grandparents' and invited her to the eleventh-grade dance at the high school they'd both attended, but the romance was never the same. Tanya went from straight A's to becoming a recluse. She tried to push herself out of bed because her grandparents were growing increasingly hurt and worried. Hoping to lift her spirits, they paid for a class trip to visit historical sites on the East Coast.

But, eventually, Tanya went back to living with her mother and started missing more school because Nancy didn't seem to care. She just kept giving Tanya notes to excuse her absences. At around this time, as Tanya recalls, doctors took a scan of her brain, diagnosed her with depression, and started giving her pills that made her feel weird. She then went to a psychiatrist who put her on antidepressants that at least helped her get up in the morning and go to sleep at night. She also went back into therapy with the social worker, to whom she'd been referred years earlier, after CPS had investigated the abuse. Tanya financially depended upon the state to support her treatment. But they sent the checks to her mom, who used them for rent instead.

Because her depression was so severe, Tanya thought that she was physically ill. She missed so many days of high school that she almost was not graduated, even though she had passing grades. Her psychology teacher, who was one of the teachers in whom she'd confided about her mother's abuse, took her under his wing and she got her diploma in June 1992. For graduation, her grandparents bought her a car, allowing her to choose between a used Honda and a new Geo Metro.

Tanya notes that she inherited her depression from both of her parents. Her mother was adopted and unable to trace her biological parents. However, Nancy, herself, was depressed. Randy was able to trace his biological parents and found a long stream of drug abuse and alcoholism in his family.

Tanya attributes her strength, as an adult, to having had only herself to rely upon in order to survive her childhood. Growing up, when dark thoughts clouded her mind, she would try to put herself in a happier place. She'd envisioned running away with her father, whom she fantasized as being heroic, or running into the woods to get away from her mother.

One day during high school, when Tanya was riding in her mom's car, she started talking about looking forward to going to college. Suddenly, Nancy got the evil look on her face that Tanya recognized as signaling the personality that was violent. Tanya got out of the car and Nancy tried to run her over. Tanya attributed this to her mother's anger and jealousy over her grandmother helping Tanya to start college.

She began studying at Green River Community College, taking classes such as the History of Art. Tests showed that she would make a good psychologist. But, she was stuck living with an absentee mother and trying to hold a job at the same time. She started missing classes.

She left Green River and went to a different community college because this one offered a class that she had failed in high school. She wanted to retake the class because she'd felt bad about it. She also took a Spanish class because she wanted to make up for what she'd missed. Tanya wanted to finish whatever she had left unfinished, so that she could get back to her original plan. She'd long dreamed of going to the University of Washington and becoming a psychologist to get a deeper understanding of her family.

By the time Tanya reached her late teens, her experiences with men throughout her childhood—from her dad to her mother's boyfriends—had left her fearful of them. The thought has occurred to her that one or more of Nancy's boyfriends may have sexually abused her. If so, she has blocked out these memories and she is glad of it. But, many other painful and frightening memories persist.

In February 1993, Tanya met Tom Rider, the man whom she would eventually marry. He was twenty-four and she was eighteen. Tanya was attending community college and working at a telemarketing job where Tom worked in a row in front of her. One of the other girls was trying to ask him out but he only had eyes for Tanya. To discourage the other girl, Tom passed Tanya a note. Tanya hadn't noticed him and she was stunned. Tom was very nervous when they began to converse, and he asked her to a party. As she remembers it, "The little child inside of him was asking me out." It was love at first sight.

Tanya soon discovered that Tom didn't live in a "good world." The party was in a rundown apartment where two guys lived, not what she expected for a first date. On their second date, Tom asked her to marry him and run off into the sunset together. But he lived with his dad in a shoddy house and didn't have a car. Besides, Tanya didn't trust men or marriage.

Still, she felt a very strong attraction to Tom and felt comfortable around him. She liked how Tom made her feel—and she had never felt this way before. Even though he wore dirty sweat pants, he seemed like a gentleman. Tanya was into looking hot and wearing Nordstrom make-up. Her grandparents had bought her a nice car, a white Honda Civic, so she wound up driving Tom around. When they'd get off work, she'd go to his house.

They'd hug in his driveway for hours, while chaos swirled around them. She lived with her volatile mom. Tom lived with his alcoholic dad. After three months, they became intimate. Tom was her first lover. "I was afraid of intimacy because of the situations I saw my mother in with men," Tanya explains. Tom had stopped his amorous advances when she needed him to, so she'd felt safe enough with him to be intimate.

Spellbound by Tom, Tanya missed a week of college and her mother jumped at the chance to tell Grandma that the young woman wasn't a perfect little princess, after all. For the first time, Tanya's grandmother became furious with her. "What are you doing with Tom? He's going nowhere," her grandmother argued. "I had high hopes for you, but you're just like your mother—dating losers!" Tanya could only say that she liked the way Tom made her feel, but that wasn't good enough. From then on, Tanya's grandmother stopped helping her pay for school, and she never forgave Tanya for shattering her illusion.

One night, Tanya went to visit Tom and found out he was at a party. She went to that address. When the door opened, Tanya saw Tom in the midst of people doing drugs and partying along with them. She was shocked and created a big scene. It hit Tanya hard when she discovered that Tom was into drugs because it reminded her of her mother's parties and her father's addiction. "Drugs took my father away from me," she says. "I learned to view drugs as the enemy." She was deeply hurt that Tom hadn't told her about the drugs, so she broke up with him.

When they broke up, Tanya began dating other men and even became intimate with a few of them but, in an effort to be honest, she told them about having left her heart with Tom. Lost in oblivion because of missing him, she shoved the other men aside. Ultimately, like a moth to a flame, Tanya couldn't resist going back to Tom. She saw the little boy underneath Tom's 'bad boy' persona, who needed rescuing from his dangerous and disappointing life. Unconsciously, she was drawn to him because she had been abandoned by her father, and was looking for a man who needed her nurturing and would, therefore, be least likely to abandon her.

Tom knew she was seeing other men. He didn't have money or a job—since telemarketing wasn't working out for him. "He was into a lot of under-the-table, bad, bad things," Tanya admits. And she'd made a pact with herself that she was never going to let alcohol or drugs become a part of her life. Tom told her that he wanted to leave his "bad" life behind and be with her, so she gave him an ultimatum. She told him that she was going to go back to her mother's apartment, and if he was serious about leaving everything behind, she wanted him to come to her that night. She returned to her mom's and slept outside in her car. But Tom never came.

The next day, he told her that the reason he hadn't come was that he'd needed to clean up some unfinished business because he didn't want anyone to hurt his dad. They headed to her mother's apartment. They had plans to get an apartment together. Meanwhile, Tom planned to sleep in his car. But, then a neighbor saw him and told the landlord, who told Tanya's mom. Nancy promptly changed the locks and ran to Grandma with this latest bit of dirt.

So, one-and-a-half years after they met, Tom and Tanya moved together into a cheap apartment in a terrible neighborhood. They didn't have much furniture, but they had each other. Tom felt bad about the way he had treated Tanya—being rude, not taking her on real dates, always making her come to him, and bringing her into his sordid life. So he tried to be a gentleman by encouraging Tanya to sleep comfortably on the daybed her grandmother had bought her years ago, while he slept on the floor.

Nancy was angry that Tanya had left her, and that she could no longer receive half the rent that the state had been paying for Tanya. She was also jealous of Tanya's brand new car. So Nancy—or Tanya's grandmother—told the state about the car. As a result, the state cut off payments to Tanya and wanted her to sell her CRX before they would help pay for her medication. Tanya didn't want to give up her car, so she stopped taking her medicine. Since then, she's tried to handle her depression on her own with health food, supplements and exercise.

Tanya got Tom a job at the telemarketing place where she was currently working, but they both decided to leave and then shifted through several other jobs—Tanya mostly working in telemarketing and Tom mostly in construction. Eventually, they were able to move into a better apartment where they lived day-by-day and paycheck-to-paycheck, trying to pay their bills and to escape the chaos of their earlier lives.

Tom's background is similar to Tanya's. His parents divorced when he was a baby. When his mother was three-quarters of the way through her daily gallon of burgundy wine, "She wished I was never born!" he recalls. Tom's mother remarried several times. When Tom was a little boy, his mother caught his stepfather at a whorehouse. When they got home, his stepfather started beating his mom. Tom pleaded with him to stop. His stepfather ignored his cries and threw him across the room. Tom grabbed the leg of the kitchen table and jumped on his back, bringing the table leg crashing down on his stepfather's head and splitting it open. His mother called 911, packed up their stuff, grabbed the kids and left. His stepfather didn't die, but this incident left scars on both of them. The insidious scars on Tom's psyche were just as painful as his stepfather's head injury.

Tom lived with his mother until he was about ten years old. It was then that she walked in on him and his twin sister trying to make pancakes. When she saw flour all over the kitchen, Tom's mother had a "breakdown" of sorts and called Tom's father to take him. Tom calls himself an "airplane baby" because he then began yearly flights between his parents, spending his summer with his mom and the rest of the year with his dad.

Fitting in with kids at school was rough. He remembers being called "Tubby Tommy," being picked on and getting into fights. When Tom got old enough to date, he had bad luck with girls. His dysfunctional relationship with his mom and his low self-esteem got in the way. Several girls played him for what they could get from him but then told him that they wanted to be "just friends," not his girlfriend. So when he met Tanya, and she looked at him with a smile in her eyes that told him she thought he was her knight in shining armor, it made him feel special.

Around the time that Tanya met and moved in with Tom, Tanya's dad and stepmom had adopted a little girl. Tanya felt replaced. Now some other little girl would get her father's love—the love he hadn't given to her. Tanya was Tom's princess now, and she demanded that he become a better person and leave "bad Tom" behind. They struggled with tough times, but they were determined that their love would see them through. Tanya had separated Tom from the unsavory life he'd led before, and Tom tried to separate Tanya from her depression by making her laugh a lot and working to replace her negative thoughts with positive ones. He soon convinced Tanya to adopt a bushy Karelian bear dog, whom they named Lady. A gentle companion and good listener, Lady quickly became Tanya's best friend.

In 1998, Tom and Tanya ran off and got married in Nevada, just as he'd asked her to do on their second date. She'd made him wait six years. She knew she loved him but she had trust issues, his background made her hesitant, and people warned her that men can become abusive after marriage. But, after Tanya had tested Tom—and she was convinced he'd proven his love—she decided it was time.

Tom bought the rings. They drove to Nevada and got a license after they arrived. When they married, in front of the courthouse, only Tom's mother and sister were there. After the ceremony, Tanya called her father, mother and grandmother. She knew they wouldn't come to the wedding because they still didn't like Tom. She was right. No one in her family was excited or happy for her.

Tom and Tanya moved around, trying to find a place where they felt loved and where they could attain the stability that kept eluding them. They tried moving to be close to Tom's family, but his mother and little sister became aggressively competitive with Tanya, whom they saw as a rival for his attention and affection. Their stay at his mom's house ended with her tossing his belongings on her porch. The message was clear: Tom's mother had crushed his long-harbored hopes that, one day, she would welcome and appreciate him.

When Tom and Tanya moved back to Washington, they started a siding and construction business, aptly named Lazarus Siding. They nurtured it, and did fairly well for five years, until some homeowners took advantage of their good hearts. Worn out, emotionally and physically, they closed their business, leaving a void in their lives.

Despite his wife's protestations, Tanya's father had come to Washington for a couple of visits and had been calling Tanya to chat. He seemed to be making an effort to make up for past mistakes. Randy tried to persuade Tanya and Tom to move near him and he offered to hire them to work for his painting company. But Tanya was afraid of becoming a victim of her father's emotional abuse and controlling behavior again. Nonetheless, they decided to visit him and check it out.

Randy bought plane tickets for them. But the visit got off to a bad start when their cell phone died and they had no way to let him know that their plane was going to be delayed. When they landed, instead of the loving greeting Tanya had looked forward to, her father was angry that they hadn't called. He remained in a sullen and hostile mood until he dropped them off at their motel. His parting words, "You're in my town now!" transformed Tanya into the scared little girl she had been when she was under his control. Tom glared at Randy and took a threatening stance as Randy sped out of the parking lot, leaving burned rubber in his tracks.

At that moment, Tanya realized that her father was probably never going to be the loving dad that she had always dreamed he would become. The next morning, they checked out of the rundown motel where Randy had left them and boarded a bus to Disney World. Randy didn't connect with them until early that evening, and it seemed to Tanya that it was more to regain control than to express his apologies and love.

Tanya called her late twenties to early thirties her "dark period." During these years, they lost their business and she lost her health, her father's love and her dog, Lady. Tanya sunk into depression again. She stopped taking care of herself and stopped eating right because the depression and their dire financial straits cast a dark cloud over her life. Eventually, she tried treating the depression on her own, with her regimen of health food, supplements and exercise, and she seemed to be gradually extricating herself from the darkness.

Then Tom's grandmother died, leaving them an inheritance. She'd wanted Tom and Tanya to have a house. They thought about opening up a health-food store, where Tom would do massage and Tanya would become a nutritionist, but they decided that such a venture was too risky. Investing in land to build a house seemed safer, so they began looking for a dream property. It took them a couple of years, but Tanya finally found one in

Shelton, Washington that they really liked. They also bought a new RV, which they would put on the property to live in during construction.

Tom and Tanya began negotiations to buy a new tract house in Maple Valley, where they would live temporarily. The plan was to sell it after awhile and use the money to finish the house they were building. Ironically, right before Tanya went missing, they had bought Tanya a new Honda Element SUV, had gotten a mortgage for their tract home in Maple Valley, and they had picked up the building permit for their dream home in Shelton. The Shelton property overlooked a beautiful inlet with whales and eagles. It seemed perfect.

Would life mirror what had happened to her as a little girl? Spoiled at times by her father and her grandparents, Tanya's happy moments almost always meant that some form of pain was coming. No sooner would something good happen, than something awful would jump out at her, like a coiled rattlesnake waiting for her to let down her guard. Whenever her father spoiled her, it meant she was in danger of being controlled by him and treated harshly by her 'evil stepmother.' Whenever her grandparents spoiled her, it meant she was in danger of being beaten by her enraged and jealous mother. Now, finally, life was good. But was it the calm before the storm?

"I've always thought about the brighter picture. I believe that, in life, people use alcohol, relationships, sex and other distractions as a way to choose to drown out hurtful aspects of their lives. And, when people have had bad things happen to them—or they've had bad parents or suffered depression or whatever—they make bad choices. I've had a hard life and faced many challenges, but I've tried to deal with them by choosing positive things— like health foods, exercise, supplements and positive thoughts—to use as my crutches. This is how I fuel my strength to fight off my weaknesses. I may have been diagnosed with depression, but I do not let it rule how I live my life. This works for me. I think it makes me a stronger person. Through these choices, and other choices that I make every day, I face my problems and have been able to break the cycle of my family history."

—*Tanya Rider*

CHAPTER ONE

8 Days

Tiny puffs of air squeeze up through my left nostril. My chest... My chest is constricted. What's wrong with me? I fight to expand my lungs, to suck in a breath. Something is pressing into my chest, holding me down. My lungs! I can't breathe! It feels like small, sandwich-bag sacks of air are hanging in my lungs. I cling to them but my body collapses forward, against my captor.

Bound on one side, I beg for release. "Let me go, you monster!" I gasp. "Where are you? I can feel you but I don't hear you! Still, I know you are there!"

I can't talk anymore. My chest is gagging, half-silencing my breathing. Everything hurts. I slow myself to suck in precious air—air for battle.

"Help me!" I scream. "Someone? Can't you hear me? Help me!"

My eyes flutter open and it seems as if all of my long dark hair is in my face. My eyelashes flutter against the tangled mess. My head is killing me and I can't hold my eyes open. They slam shut, but the images linger.

Where am I? Why is my head hanging at this weird angle? I am sideways, I can tell. And I feel an awful, constant pressure digging into my body. God, it hurts. I struggle again to take a breath. I can only take in a tiny wisp of air but it is filled with pain that shoots through every fiber of my body. Still, I need more air. With a weak exhale, I feel a little cloud of steam drift onto my cheek as I hang there, strangled by my captor. Sweet drool runs out of the corner of my mouth.

With my right arm, I reach out blindly. I want to feel my surroundings. I feel hard curves, twisted forms, raw edges, and a strange, soft pillow—all of it dotted with bits of broken glass. I cannot tell what these shapes represent, but it is a mess. Where am I? Right against my chest, my hand runs into something, an object, an arc, like a hard, circle shaped hose. I run my fingers slowly across it. Can it be? A steering wheel? Each breath cuts through my breastbone and I strain to pull in air. I run my hand along the thing, try to assure myself that it really is a car's steering wheel.

Tom Rider was tired, always tired. He and Tanya worked hard, and that's about all they did. Like ships in the night, they didn't even see each other much. He barely had time to nap, let alone spend much time with Tanya, because she worked two jobs herself and her shifts were opposite his. Pretty much, they only got to see each other when their days off coincided. Their lifestyle was kind of lonely, but they were determined. They had set their sights on their goal—their dream home—and they were working hard to get it.

They'd had a quick conversation the night before. Tanya had called after ten on Wednesday night, before she started her nightshift. Tom had to work late so he was spending the night at work, and he'd already crashed. When Tanya called, she woke him up.

"What're you doing?" she asked.

"Sleeping," he grumbled.

Tanya knew his sleep was precious so she immediately hung up, and then she worked the night shift at Fred Meyer, up in Bellevue. She would have gotten home after Tom was a few hours into his day.

Open your eyes, Tanya! I squint. Everything is blurry. Where are my glasses? My head hurts so much and I am so tired. All I want to do is to close my eyes, go back to sleep. But I don't know where I am. Where am I? What is that flashing light in front of me? I open my eyes to let in a bit more light, and I see the dashboard with its yellow and orange car controls. I reach my hand to the fluorescent image, but it is beyond my reach. I turn my head to the left and I can see the black molding inside my side window. I see glimpses of the color of my car, the beautiful blue of my wonderful new car.

My eyes snap shut again as I erupt with a cough, dislodging saliva and blood from a corner of my mouth. Oh, it hurts so much! I spit out the oily blood, not knowing how precious those drops of moisture would become.

I try to breathe, but my chest feels stuck. It won't expand and I can't get air. I don't understand. I exercise all the time and I'm in such great shape, why can't I breathe? I pull my eyes open again. I reach up to my face to brush the messy mop of hair aside, and then I see that my fingertips are bloody. I touch my forehead again and it stings. It is raw. I check my fingers. More blood.

It starts to make sense. It is the steering wheel of my car, my beautiful Honda, the first car I ever bought new! But everything is broken and twisted and I am trapped inside it. I am pinned against the steering wheel and I can't see much but the deflated air bag, which blocks my view. I press at it, try to move it aside.

Oh, my body hurts! My left shoulder, my God, the pain is horrible! My arm is hanging from my side at an odd angle against the door. I can't move my arm. I don't even want to wiggle my fingers. The pain is unbelievable. Oh, my God, the pain! It's searing! My left side feels broken, disconnected. My left clavicle and my left shoulder are burning with pain that is deep, intense, in the bone and in the joint.

I can see out, through the broken window, but I can't make sense of it. Where am I? I see branches and leaves. Everywhere, all around me, blackberry bushes push in through the broken windows and up against the glass. I catch the aroma of the cedar trees, so nice, fresh.

Something is applying pressure, holding me against my will. So tight! I am trapped, pinned. It's my seat belt. I'm cramped and I can't get a decent breath of oxygen into my lungs. I try to suck in a breath but the air seems to go right through me. My chest hurts so much as the air stings my insides.

I try to free myself but I can't reach the seatbelt release. Clawing with my right hand, I feel metal. Then, my fingertips make it to the edge. With all of my mental and physical energy—everything I have—I command my fingers to take back my freedom, to pull upward on the metal. But I lose. The strap is so tight. It cuts into my body, pressing like a piece of metal. I wish I'd bought seat-belt covers to soften them. My body hurts, everywhere that my seat belt holds me—my left shoulder to my right hip and across my pelvis—it all feels bruised. I wish I could get my seat belt off!

How did I get here? What happened?

The driver's door presses into my side and it hurts so much right there, at my ribs and hip. My abdomen is bruised and swollen and I can tell that several of my ribs are fractured or cracked. My leg is trapped, pressed between the door, the seat, and the underside of the dashboard. I can tell I have little if any circulation in my leg and it worries me. Will I lose my leg? What if I can't walk again?

My head hurts and throbs. I feel as if I've been shot in the head! I just want to close my eyes and rest. Maybe, if I go to sleep, I will find out that this isn't real. It's just a bad dream. Yes, it must be a nightmare. I know! I will wake up soon and be thankful that it was all a dream.

On Thursday, as usual, Tom put in a full day at SoundBuilt. After he got off work, he put in a couple of hours on a side job, earning a few extra bucks by clearing blackberry bushes from a piece of property for a real estate agent. After that, Tom ran home to shower and then went to work at a pizza parlor until midnight. By the time he got home, Tom was dead tired. Tanya already would have left for her night job. At least, that was the routine. That's what Tom assumed.

I open my eyes. Have I been asleep again? I hear the trees, flowing in the wind somewhere out there, but I can't see them. It is like a meadow outside, so cool and fresh. I'm down, in a bramble of bushes and I can just make out scraps of blue sky through the shrubbery. It's windy. The wind is blowing the bushes and sometimes, with a gust out there, I feel a slip of wind on my face as a wayward strand of hair wisps past my cheek. With the breeze, I can smell the cedar, fresh, clean and nice. I decide to think about the cedar, but...

Something smells bad. My goodness, it's blood! There's blood everywhere—my blood. I smell pee, too. Oh, my gosh, I think I peed my pants. How awful! I peed in my pants? I suddenly notice that my bladder is full and I feel like I have to pee more. What will I do? I can't go anywhere to pee. I can't get out to go to the bathroom. Oh, God, I have to just lie here and pee myself? How horrible! Someone help me! Help me get out of here! I just want to get up! I pull on my seat belt, claw at the clasp. I can't unfasten it. It won't come off. Oh, my gosh. What will I do?

I hear cars driving nearby. I suck all the air I can into my lungs and yell, "Help me! I'm trapped, here. Please, help me!" I don't hear anyone stop. They must not hear me. I knock on the window. Can't they hear that?

I see a bee buzzing around the blackberry shrub near my fractured windshield. It starts to wander inside my car and I wave my hand to shoo it away. I turn my head, look to the side. I see bugs flying around me, inside my car. Oh, God! What about critters? What if any critters find me? I am afraid of snakes! What if snakes come in here? Calm down, calm down. I don't hear any animals. It is quiet outside, except for that breeze. I am okay. I will be okay. If any animals come near me, I can use my hand to scare them away.

My stomach growls. I'm hungry. I wish I had something to eat. I don't know when I last had something to eat, I don't even know how long I've been stuck here, but I am so hungry! Have I been here for a few hours? Why doesn't someone come?

It's getting cold. I am cold. I notice that there are shadows in the bushes, and inside my car. The sun must be behind clouds because it's not as bright as it had been. I search for the bits of blue sky but they are no longer blue. Oh, God! The sky is yellowish orange and the air is wet and heavy. God, help me! The sun is setting. Oh, God, what will I do when it gets dark?

God, you are my rock and my shield. I'm so frightened but, with you by my side, I know I am safe. I trust you, God. Please help me to trust your will completely. You know all things before they happen. Please protect me, God. Be near me and guide others to me. No amount of suffering will ever take away my love for you, God. Be near me, God. Be near me...

My stomach growls, yet again. I am so hungry. Why isn't anyone helping me? I do not understand. I'm right here! I am so mad! I start to cry and, as the tears well up, I feel the urge to give in to them, to let go, to pour out my frustration and rage. But my abdomen and chest hurt. I whimper. I need to rest. I close my eyes.

I wake up and see an eerie blue light, glowing in the darkness. It's my cell phone. Where is it? My phone! Desperate, I reach out for it, but I can't reach anything beyond my own body. I try to shift myself up to my right, but I am pinned in and the left side of my body is in agony. I am broken. I know I am broken. Oh, my God, the pain! I cannot move. I settle back down, resting my head down against the seat belt as my ripped body presses against the door below me. It hurts. It hurts so much. I close my eyes and try to breathe. Just think about breathing. In and out. Slowly now. Breathe slowly, smoothly. In and out...

It is dark but I am still thirsty. Can't I just have some food, something to drink? Please, someone, help me! Tom, bring me some water! My head is hurting in a different way and I know that it is from dehydration. The pain is blinding and I can't think. I just want to get out of here, to find some food and water. I am so tired. I want to go to sleep, but it is so cold.

I wake up and it is light out, thank God. My throat is so dry, scratchy. I want to clear my throat, but I can't muster any air or saliva. My tongue is stuck to the roof of my mouth and it feels like a brick. I want a drink of water! I want food! My stomach hurts, I'm so hungry, and I feel weak. My gut cramps up in a weird way. At least, I'm too dehydrated to pee anymore. Oh, that's what stinks in here! The air is thick and stale and the smell so foul, as the stink of my own wastes and blood fills my little space. It's like an outhouse, like I'm living in my own outhouse, surrounded by my waste.

I try again, banging on the window, yelling at the cars that whir by so fast. I try to shift, reposition my body to reach the latch yet another time, another way. I claw at the seatbelt clasp and my fingertips burn from trying to get that clasp free, but I will do anything to escape this prison. I have a new pain when I move my right arm. It's bad. It aches with deep, intense pain in my armpit. I have to think again about trying to fight that damned clasp. It hurts so much.

How long have I been here? I feel like I am encased in a metal tomb but, still, it won't give up its twisted metal grip on me. I try again to contort my broken body against the steady weight of twisted and jagged metal and the restraint of the seatbelt, but it hurts so much more when I move and my right arm is less help than before. I feel blurry. I don't know what to do. Should I give up? The world goes black again.

On Friday morning, just like every day, Tom woke up at five o'clock in their makeshift bed on the floor. They'd lived in an RV during construction and had only recently moved into the house, which was still bare bones, so Tom and Tanya didn't even have a bed. Tom got up, showered, and headed off to work. As the morning went on, he didn't hear from Tanya. He figured she didn't call because she needed to sleep. They always needed sleep.

Sleep only lasts so long. I wake up and try again and again— knocking on the window, clawing at the clasp, pulling at the seatbelt. Is it futile? I press against the pain and try and try and try until I am exhausted. I let my eyes close so I can rest my body, my aching head.

I jump. The phone is ringing! My cell phone is ringing! I look for the blue light. Where is the phone? I twist and pull my broken chest and press my body against the confinement of the seatbelt, trying to reach it, desperate to reach it. Panic overtakes reason. I can't reach it! I have to reach it! God, please let me reach it! "Tom!" I scream. "Tom, I'm here!" The phone stops. I cuss and yell and tap my foot on the floorboard. Oh, my God! Tom, I'm here! I want to hear his voice of reassurance! I want to call 911! I want help!

I think about my dog, Lady, who has comforted me countless times in the past. Lady is such a good friend and she means so much to me. Where is Lady? Lady, are you with me? I love you, Lady.

I am hungry and thirsty. What's the last thing I ate or drank? I know! I got off work in the morning and stopped at Whole Foods. I felt so gross, after working all night at my dirty job. What did I buy? I usually trust whatever my body's craving and buy something to have later because I'd usually need to go to sleep when I got home. I'm sure I got a bottle of water, which is always my first priority. Since we're building our house, we don't have a fridge so, whenever I stop at Whole Foods, I'd usually get pancakes, make a salad in the deli, or sprinkle cheese on scrambled eggs...

I am so hungry, I feel weak. I don't understand why I can't have some eggs and a bottle of water. My lips are cracking and I am tired. I feel blurry.

I need help! I realize that I need to call for help. I reach through the steering wheel and pick up my phone from the dashboard. I call 911.

"911," she says. "What is your emergency?"

"I went off the road and I need help!"

"That's stupid!" says the dispatcher, laughing at me before she hangs up.

I am so mad! I can't believe it. I want to tell Tom, so I call him.

"Hey," he answers. He sounds happy and casual.

"What the hell, Tom?" I yell at him, furious.

"What do you mean?" he asks.

"Why are you taking so long to come and get me?"

He doesn't answer. The line goes dead. In an instant, the phone rings.

The phone! Where is my phone? I see the blue light, over there. I try, but I cannot reach it. I am pinned in my seat and I cannot reach my cell phone. I claw at the seatbelt until my fingertips are raw and burning, then I pound on the window and yell. Finally, I am tired. I let my eyes close.

"Hi, Lady!" I say. She looks startled but then she smiles at me. She has a cute smile and her teeth are white. Her tongue is hanging out and it glistens with wet saliva. I look out my window, where there's just a bramble of bushes, but I see a reflection of Lady on the window. I realize that she's sitting in the other seat, looking out the front window at the scenery, and then she turns her head in front of me and smiles again. "Aw, Lady," I say, reaching for her. "You're always right here!"

I am cold. The night is cold and I shiver. It is harder to rest at night because the animal sounds scare me. My adrenaline flows and, besides, it is cold. I am wide-eyed, staring into darkness. I hear the brush rustle, as a critter moves through the darkness. Maybe it's a squirrel. Or a rat. What if it's a raccoon? They are mean, so I hope it is not a raccoon. A car passes on the road and the red of their tail lights flashes in the night above me as the animal scurries away. I reach for the clasp and try again.

Forest animals make a lot of noise at dawn. A large bird lands on the hood of my bright blue SUV. Sideways, I see his head, his beak. His head is white with a little black streak. I don't see the rest of him but I know that he is a bald eagle. He looks at me with yellow-green eyes and is very interested in me. I've never been so close to a bald eagle. He stays with me. His skinny legs try to keep their grip on the hood of my car. Now, he seems more interested in getting off the hood, and he is not looking at me. He's looking down, in front of the car. He is focusing on what's below and thinking about going. Why does he get to hop off the hood? I'm glad that he doesn't. He stays with me. I look into his eyes and thank him in my thoughts.

SoundBuilt was Tom's Monday-through-Friday job so, on Saturday, he had the luxury of sleeping until eight o'clock. He planned to spend the day tackling those blackberry bushes. The agent who was handling the property needed the wetlands cleared fast and Tom was squeezing in the project between his regular job and his pizza job. At nine that morning, Tom was working on the blackberries when his phone rang. It was Tanya's boss at Fred Meyer.

"Is everything alright?" she asked.

"'Course," Tom said. "Why?"

"Well, Tom, Tanya hasn't been at work for the last two shifts and—"

"*What?*" Tom said, shocked. "What are you talking about? That's not like Tanya!"

"I know Tom," she said. "She hasn't been at work and she hasn't called and it's not like her, so I just wanted to make sure everything's alright."

"*What?*" Tom repeated, his mind reeling as he jumped gears from the physical work to contemplating what he was hearing. "When is the last time you saw her?"

"She left Thursday morning, around nine," the woman said, concern growing in her voice. "And, Tom, she's not answering her phone."

Tom's mind went into overdrive. *When's the last time I called her? When's the last time I talked to her?*

"I'll try to get hold of her as soon as I hang up, and I'll have her call you," Tom promised. "Is there a number you can give me?" Standing out in the bushes, Tom wrote the number on his hand and then ran to his truck.

He called Tanya's cell phone. No answer. He called again and, again, she didn't answer. After a few tries, he left a message. He climbed in his truck and started to drive, without really thinking about where he was going. Tom thought to call Tanya's boss at her second job, at the Nordstrom Rack. He found out that Tanya hadn't been scheduled to work the day before, Friday, but that, at the moment, she was late for her shift—and she hadn't called. Tanya's boss, like everyone, knew that Tanya would never miss work and not call in. That's just not *her*.

Worry flooded his senses. *No way* would Tanya miss work. If she had, he would have seen her at home! Where could she *be*?

Finally, Tom realized that Tanya was missing—and that she had *already been* missing for thirty-six hours. *Thirty-six hours!* Starting to search for her, Tom knew that this gap in time would be a great disadvantage. Far too much time had passed. Their crazy life had gotten in the way. While they were both working two jobs, she had disappeared from the radar and he had kept on working, assuming that everything was going according to plan.

I am hungry—hungrier than I have ever been. I didn't know a person could be this hungry. I know that it is making me weak. I look at my wrist and see that I am even thinner than I was. I don't understand. I am so healthy, how can I feel so sick? I don't deserve to be this sick, since I am so careful about eating well, choosing organic foods, exercising every day.

But I am so tired. I cannot exercise today. I am going to rest. Right after I get a drink of water. That's all I want, a drink of water. My tongue sticks to my cheeks and the roof of my mouth. My lips are cracked and when I try to move them, I feel them rip and bleed.

Tom ended up at home. He ran into the house and darted through every room, searching for her.

"Tanya!" he called. "*Tanya?* Are you home?" His panic grew. Time started to lose meaning. He jumped back in his truck to drive the routes to her jobs. While driving, he called 911 and asked for the Highway Patrol. They told him that they'd had no reports of Tanya and no accidents that matched her car or name. Tom called all the local hospitals, but no one had seen her. What else could he do? Again, he called 911.

"Bellevue Police Department."

"My wife is missing," Tom choked out.

"Sir," the dispatcher asked, "when was the last time she was seen?"

"Thursday," he swallowed. "She left work at nine in the morning, after her shift."

"Did anyone see her leave?"

"I don't know yet," Tom said. "I'm on my way to her second job, at the Factoria Nordstrom Rack. She's missed her last two shifts there. She hasn't accessed our accounts and all she has is her Nordstrom Visa card. I can't check that one because I'm not on it."

"When you get there, we'll send over an officer to take your statement."

"No problem," Tom said, grateful. "I'll be there in five minutes."

After Tom arrived, he only waited about five minutes before a Bellevue police officer found him. Nordstrom personnel escorted them into a room in the security department.

"So," the police officer asked Tom, "when was the last time you heard from your wife?"

"Around ten PM on Wednesday," Tom said. "She called me when she was leaving for work. I was staying at work that night because I had an early morning homeowner walk scheduled and I had to work late to get it ready."

"What did she say?" the officer asked. "Was there any kind of fight? Did she say anything that might make you think she was leaving you?"

"No," Tom said, his heart sinking. "All she asked was, 'What are you doing?' I said, 'sleeping' and she hung up. It was quite normal for her to just check in to hear my voice."

"So she just hung up?" the officer asked.

"We've been married for a long time," Tom said, "and she's been mad at me at *least* half of it. We fight. We're married."

"So, you're sure she didn't just leave you? Like she'd had enough, kind of thing?"

Tom *knew* that Tanya wouldn't leave him—at least not before giving him a reason. But where was she? He couldn't imagine where she was or what she was doing, and all these questions about her leaving got to him. "But, if she'd left," he reasoned, "she would have taken some—if not *all*—of the money! She didn't take anything except her Nordstrom Visa."

"So when was the last time you know where she was?"

Tom told him that the last he could track was that she'd left her job at Fred Meyer in Bellevue at nine in the morning. "If she was using her card since then," he added, "I can't check that and that's why I need to get a case started so you can check."

"Which card? Her Nordstrom card?" the officer asked.

"Yes," Tom said. "That's the only card she has with her and, like I said, I'm not on it so they won't tell me anything."

"Wait here," the office said. "I'll check a few things out and be right back."

Tom waited, talking with Tanya's boss, who thought it was not in Tanya's nature to do this. "I've only known her a short time," he said. "But she seems to be very dependable."

Tom asked the manager if they'd noticed anyone who stood out, who seemed strange, but the manager said that they keep a close eye out for that kind of thing and saw no signs of it.

"Thanks," Tom said. "Please, if you hear from her, please call me."

The officer came back into the room, looking at his notes. "We've found video footage of Tanya getting into her car at the end of her shift and driving out toward the highway," he said. "My sergeant has informed me that our involvement has to end. You have to contact King County Police to follow up since our jurisdiction ended when she left work. Since we have evidence that she left our jurisdiction of her own volition, we have to hand you off to King County."

"So, you're telling me I have to call 911 again once I get back into Maple Valley?" Tom asked, incredulous. He felt helpless and frustrated. "Can I ask *why* I have to wait?"

"Because with cell phones, 911 calls connect you to the office based on the tower your call goes through, and not based on your phone number," the officer explained. "This way, you get the right department to assist you."

Tom headed for the door—and for Maple Valley.

Finally, again, my eyes close and I drift off into peaceful unconsciousness. But, soon, my phone rings. It snaps me back to my agony of excruciating pain. Where is my phone? Tom! Are you calling me, Tom? I want to answer but I can't reach the phone. I feel a wave of dizziness and I panic. I flail with my hand to grab the steering wheel. Finally, the dizziness calms.

When he got home, he called 911 again, connecting this time with the King County Police Dispatch and Communications Center.

"My wife is missing," he said. "And the Bellevue police said I need to file a missing person report with you."

The operator didn't sound very concerned. "Have you checked the hospitals and jails?" he asked. To Tom, the operator seemed cold, as if he was reading a script. Tom didn't want to answer as his anger was rising.

"Yes, *of course*, I checked the hospitals," he finally spat out. "And the State Patrol. Those were the first calls I made! I haven't checked the jails but, if my wife was in jail, she would've called me for bail money. My wife's *not* in jail. She's never been in trouble. The only contact she's had with the police is being stopped for *speeding*!"

Tom's helplessness was making his hostility rise. He had to work to hold it back as he spoke with the operator and it took more patience than he knew he had.

"You can't file a report until you have checked all the jails," the operator insisted. "So, I need you to do that and then call back." With that, the operator hung up.

Tom was furious, but he used the energy to do what he needed to do. He ran upstairs and got on the Internet, to search for phone numbers for the jails. On the websites, he found out that he could conduct a prisoner search online. He checked all the jails' records for any record of "Tanya Rider." Over and over, from every jail, the result was the same: "No Record Found."

Trying for the second time to report Tanya's disappearance to the King County Police, Tom punched the numbers 911 in his phone again. As it rang on the other end, he yelled at his handset, *"Why won't you just do your job and file a report so we can start searching for my wife?"* All he wanted was for them to start looking for Tanya! As the stress tore at his sanity, he felt himself losing control. He felt his old self coming back—the angry man he used to be, before Tanya. He didn't want to be that guy again but why, he wondered, were they were making such a simple task so damned difficult?

The operator answered. "911 what are you reporting?"

"I called earlier," Tom said, sucking in a measure of calmness and patience. "My wife is missing. I called all the hospitals, the jails, the morgue, the State Patrol. No one has any information on her. She is missing.

"Okay, have you called her friends and family?"

What the hell? Tom thought. *Every damned time I call, they come up with something else for me to do! Would it kill them to tell me all of this the first time I call?* But he didn't say it. He kept it in, sucked in yet another breath and gathered his patience. "She doesn't really have any friends," he said. "And she doesn't talk to her family."

"I can't file a report until you check with her family," said the operator. "She's an adult, and she can go where she wants."

"So you're telling me that because she's an adult she has the right to die?"

"Call back after you check with her family," the operator instructed. "Goodbye," he added, before the line went dead.

My phone rings again. It stops. It rings. It stops. I want to answer. Oh, God, I want to answer! Come and help me! Come and find me and free me from this hell! I cry, but no tears come.

I want this nightmare to end, just end—quickly end. I think about my mortality. How long will I have to wait until death claims me? When will I finally die and be spared from this hell?

Tom called Tanya's family and found out that, just as he had suspected, they hadn't spoken in a long time. Again, he punched the numbers into the phone.

"911, what are you reporting?"

"My wife is missing and I've called all the jails, hospitals, friends and family," Tom said. "And no one has seen her. She hasn't touched our accounts."

"Okay, let me ask you a few questions. Does she suffer from any mental disorders?"

"No," Tom answered. "She was diagnosed with depression but she's treating it."

"What type of medication does she take?"

"She treats it with her diet and staying away from non-organic foods."

"Then she doesn't meet our criteria for a search."

What? Tom was shocked. Tanya was missing, had been for two days, and she didn't meet their criteria? He felt panicky as his adrenaline rose. "So, what you are telling me is, unless she's dead you don't *care?*"

"She's an adult and she can go when and where she wants," the operator said bluntly and without emotion. "And she doesn't have to tell you or anyone."

What? Tom screamed inside. He felt the darker side of his own nature launch a full scale assault. His insides seethed. Trying to control his temper, he clenched his teeth with unhealthy force. *Think before speaking,* he told himself, mustering all of his willpower. *Do not lose it now,* he thought, *or you could lose her for good.*

"So," Tom said, "what you're saying is that, unless she's dead, you don't care?"

"With no evidence of foul play, I can't start an investigation," said the operator, coolly.

"*What* criteria?" Tom demanded. "She's *missing!* This isn't like her! She never misses work and if she was going to leave, she would've taken some money—if not all of it!" As he finished speaking, his internal voice screamed, *What in the hell do they pay you for, you moron?* But reason prevailed and he swallowed hard, leaving his feelings unsaid.

"She doesn't meet the criteria for a search," the operator told him simply.

The operator's rigidity and lack of concern at once emotionally drained and enraged Tom. He couldn't take it. "How are you going to feel if she dies tomorrow and you could have helped?" Tom blurted out, struggling to push some calm into his voice. "How is *that* going to fit your criteria?"

"Unless there's evidence of foul play or she's a minor or on medication for a mental disorder, she doesn't meet the criteria for a missing person," the operator said, sounding a little irritated. "She's an adult. She can go where she pleases and we do not have to look for her."

"Arghhh, this *can't* be happening!" Tom said, as his rage boiled up and over. "What the *hell* do we have the police for—if not for *this*? Aren't you supposed to 'protect and serve'? Why the hell is that written on all your fucking cars?" The longer the conversation continued, the more he struggled with himself. *This isn't right*, he thought. *This just isn't right!*

Tom needed someone to listen so he looked online for news contacts and called the news tip line at Channel 13. The Q13 tip line reporter told Tom that, without a case number, they couldn't run the story. Tom explained that Tanya did not meet the police department's criteria, so the police refused to open a case. The reporter offered to check about the criteria with the Sheriff's office and see what he could do. He said he'd call back.

Maybe I have missed a solution. Can I figure out a way to escape this captivity? If there is a way, I will find it! I will not be a victim!

Is this even real? Is my mind failing me?

God, I do not think I can do this. Please save me, God. Please protect me. I am not strong enough without you. I want so desperately to get out. Please, Lord, guard my mind, heart and body from the evil snares of the devil. God, I give you all that I am for you to fulfill your will. You always said ask and you shall receive. Lord, I'm asking—no, I'm begging—please help me. I need you. I cannot do this. I believe you can, God. Please do so, according to your will.

Tom called 911 again.

"911 what are you reporting?" said an operator who didn't sound familiar.

"My wife has been missing for three days now," Tom said. "I've called the jails, hospitals, family, State Patrol and the morgues. I've checked all of our accounts. She hasn't accessed any money. The only thing I can't check is her Nordstrom Visa because I'm not on that account, so they won't tell me anything. All her bankcards are at home. She has two checks that aren't cashed on the railing upstairs and..."

"Can I have her name and date of birth?"

"Tanya, that's T-A-N-Y-A, Rider, that's R-I-D-E-R." He told the operator Tanya's birthdate.

"And what was she wearing the last time you saw her?"

"Black slacks and a white blouse," Tom said. "I found a tape of her leaving work the day she disappeared. She was leaving from her overnight shift at Fred Meyers."

"Can you tell me what she was driving?"

"A blue Honda Element. Brand new, 2007, with a paper plate in the window."

"Can you tell me anything that can distinguish it from any other car of its kind?"

"Silver running boards and all the upgrades available."

During the interview, the operator gave Tom a case number, 07-284-580, and explained that they would list her and that the listing would go out countywide, statewide and countrywide, so that, if Tanya was found and an agency ran her name—anywhere in the country—they would learn that she was missing.

After they concluded the call, the operator called back, asking for the vehicle identification number (VIN) from Tanya's car. Tom found the number and gave it to the operator, but they had a little mix-up understanding the letters among the digits over the telephone. Finally, the operator found the car's record.

"I got it," the operator said. "2007 Honda. Anyway, I found it. That's great. Okay."

"It'd be better if you found *her*," Tom said.

"It really would," said the operator. "I think we're gonna go ahead and send an officer out to talk to you about this."

Thank God, Tom thought. He felt as if he'd finally reached an operator with a heart.

I think God hears my prayers with tears of His own, as I hear a single sound in the brush. A plop. Then, a second later, I hear another. Then another and another and another. In a moment, I feel it—blessed water, sprinkling and then raining down on my tomb. But it doesn't reach me. I reach out my hand toward the broken windshield but can't get my hand out far enough. Some precious drops of moisture splash into the interior of the car and I wipe them with my fingers, raising a smear of moisture to my lips.

When the King County Police officer arrived, Tom met him in the driveway.

"Are you Mr. Rider?" the officer asked.

"Yes, I am," Tom said. "My wife's missing."

"When was the last time you saw her?"

"When she left for work, she called me to see what I was doing," Tom explained. "That's the last I heard from her."

"When was that?"

"The nineteenth, around ten PM," Tom said. "She was going to work. She asked what I was doing. I said sleeping and she hung up."

"And you didn't do anything that made her angry and maybe cause her to want to leave you?"

"I don't know," Tom said. "We've been together for a long time and she gets mad at me, but she didn't say anything to make me *think* she was mad."

"How long have you been together?" the officer asked.

"Sixteen years this February," said Tom. "We've been married for about ten years this October third and we're building a house and buying this one. If she was going to leave, she would have taken the money. She hasn't touched it, so I know something's wrong."

"Do you know what she was wearing when she left?"

"Black slacks and a white blouse," Tom reported. "The Bellevue Police and I found video of her getting into her car, so they said I had to file in King County because that's where we live."

"You say she got in her car? What makes you think something happened?"

"Because she never got home and didn't go to work. That's not like her. Something happened between there and home."

"What kind of car was it?"

"Blue Honda Element, 2007. She was on tape at nine AM, getting in it and driving away from the Bellevue Fred Meyers."

"And that was on the twentieth?"

"Yes," Tom said. "That's why Bellevue said it was no longer in their jurisdiction and I would have to file a report here."

"I think we have what we need for now," the officer said. "I'll write this up and get you a card."

"Do you want to search the house?" Tom offered. "Anything you need, you don't need to waste time with a warrant. You have my permission. My life's an open book. I have nothing to hide. And I don't want you wasting resources looking at me when you could be looking for her."

"Okay, if you'll wait here I'll take a look around and come back out."

Tom waited in the driveway while the officer searched the house.

"Those are her checks on the railing?"

"Yes, and that's her bankcard on the counter," Tom said. "All she has with her is her Nordstrom Visa and I can't check it because I'm not on it. But, if you guys could check it, then we'll know if, well, if someone stole it or not."

"Well," the officer said, "I can't make those decisions. I'll turn this over to the sergeant and he'll make the call on whether it goes to a detective."

"So you mean you might not investigate, after all this?" Tom asked. "What do I have to do?"

"It is out of my hands," the officer sighed. "I just take the report."

"Well, you do what you have to and I'll do what I need to," Tom said. At least he had a case number so he could get the story out there. He thought that, maybe, some attention would force the police to do their job.

Tom called Channel 13 News, which had called the Sheriff's office about the missing persons case criteria. Can it be that that phone call tipped the scales and made them open the case?

Through the darkness again and again, my phone rings and stops, rings and stops. I want to answer it but it is somewhere over there. I can't reach it, can't even find it. My mind is foggy. If only I could reach the phone! If only I could reach the phone. If only! But I cannot. I am trapped here, stuck here, abandoned here. What if no one comes to save me? What if they never find me? How long can I survive, anyway? I have been without water for... I don't even know how long. I have been unconscious a lot. I think I have gone through two nights, but I am not sure.

Saturday night, Tom didn't know what to do with himself. He just sat at home, waiting. *Tanya*, he thought, *where are you?* When it got dark, he walked out of his house and down the driveway, to the street. he moseyed down their street and stood into the night, waiting, until morning came.

I am hungry. I had been so healthy that, maybe, my body doesn't have a lot of fat stores. I worry, but I hope that my healthy diet has given me the strength to endure this. Still, I think about food. I want food as much as I want water. My hunger and thirst add to the agony of the searing pain from my broken body. Then, my worry grows. Other things start to happen with my body, things I don't understand. My heart seems fluttery, with an irregular heartbeat. Why is my heart pounding like this? It's not like I'm exercising or anything. It's not like I had coffee with my breakfast. Oh, breakfast. I want food. But I feel dizzy and a little nauseous. Oh, my stomach feels so icky. How can I feel nausea when I haven't eaten anything? I am worried. I don't understand it.

I am floating in and out, conscious and then dreaming. Sometimes I do not know the difference. I think I am dying but God helps me to survive one more moment, one more hour. I decide that I am not trapped in a desperate situation, pinned behind the wheel of my car. Instead, I drift above my body. I float off, happily, above the beautiful mountains with snow capped peaks, above the beautiful Northwest greenery with its azaleas and ferns and grasses. Lady takes me on a serene sightseeing tour of idyllic landscapes bathed in light, away from misery.

I am back in my body. I am tired and dizzy. I don't know what to think. Why don't they come? Why doesn't Tom come?

The dizziness grows and then it sweeps over me. I close my eyes and wipe my face, avoiding my left eyebrow, which still has an open wound.

Opening my eyes, I run my hand through my hair, brushing it away from my face. Several hairs cling to my hand and I have no way to wipe them off. I feel sick to my stomach. Oh, God, it's bad. I feel my stomach swell up in me as. No! No, no, no! I don't want to throw up! But I am not in control. I face the window below my left side and try to press my face forward a little as I throw up. The vomit lands near the front of the side window. The heaving contraction of my gut and my chest makes everything hurt so badly, I can't think. I throw up again and the vomit splats all over the window at my side. I am spinning. It stinks. I can't handle it.

A detective called. She was in charge of Tanya's case and this was her first call. "I need a print out of all your accounts," she said.

Tom told her, as he'd told everyone so far, that the only card Tanya had with her was her Nordstrom Visa, and that he hadn't set up his online password yet so he had no access to that account.

"Where's the account?" she asked. "And how do you access it?"

Tom gave her their account numbers and all the information he could. He also provided his social security number and his PIN numbers, so she could check out everything for herself. He *wanted* her to. He insisted that the detective search the house and even take his computer, to prove that he wasn't involved with her disappearance in any way. He told them that they didn't need to get a warrant and that he wanted to be as open with them as he possibly could. He *pleaded* with the police to follow up on *every* lead, and he prayed that they would eliminate him as a suspect as quickly as possible, so that, then, they would move on to investigate more productive leads.

I wake up cold, so cold. My fingers and arms, legs and toes feel so cold and my heart gives a little flutter and then I feel some hard, pounding beats. I know a lot about health, but I do not understand what is happening inside my body. I just want to rest. I want to sleep and dream, but I'm angry and I want to cry. I don't have the strength, just a lame attempt, a whimper. I talk to Tom inside my head. I pray to God. I drift out above the blackberry bushes, away from the smells in my car, up to tops of the cedar trees.

"Come with me, Lady," I say inside my head. "Let's go for a ride."

But I can't find Lady. I don't know where she is.

"Tom?" I say in the silence of my mind. "Do you know where Lady is?"

Tom doesn't know where Lady is but, he says, "I love you."

"Well, I love you too," I think I say. "So why don't you come and get me?"

But Tom doesn't answer. He will come, I think.

My gut twists and turns and I feel sick again, but it is not my stomach this time. I have to go to the bathroom! I start crying. I have always worked hard to keep my life clean and orderly and, here I am, sick in my pants. Locked in my seat, fully clothed, I have diarrhea. The fresh smell is horrible and I am in agony.

I drift away again. I see myself hovering over our property in Shelton, where we had built our house, a nice home on a double lot overlooking a beautiful bay. During construction, we had lived in an RV that had air conditioning. I liked that, though I am so cold right now, I do not understand why! The RV was small, but I was happy, being so close to Tom. We know that we can conquer any challenges. We can do anything!

Facing my situation in the car, I see and smell the same horror. I keep trying to pound on the window, claw at the clasp. I try them again and again. I do not care if I have tried them a thousand times. I do not care if they have failed a thousand times. I must keep trying, even if it is futile. What else am I going to do? All I can do is choose to erase everything that binds me. I can give in and let go, but I do not want to. I have dreams to live for, so failure is not an option. I must will myself to live.

After the detective left, Tom worked around the property. It was mindless labor that he needed to do, but he only did it to keep his tortured mind occupied for a little while. Tom also worked on flyers and tried to raise money for a reward. He knew that he needed to do all he could to add to the media stories every day, so that Tanya's disappearance would stay in front of the public—and so that the public would keep the pressure on the police.

I hear a sound. I can't make sense of it, though it seems familiar. I think I should know what it is. It comes from up above me, a vibrating hum that gets louder until there's a red glow, and then the red light fades away as the sound becomes fainter. But, soon, it happens again. And again. Then it happens again but this time, the noise gets louder as a white light gets brighter and brighter and, then, the light turns to red and the noise and red light both fade away. I don't understand it.

I don't know where I am. I am in a box full of broken stuff and the box is surrounded by bushes. I can't get out and I don't know why. Why can't I get out? Why can't I move and why does everything hurt me? My head hurts so badly and my left shoulder is burning with pain—for that matter, my whole left side hurts me. I can't seem to move my legs and my back hurts. I'm stuck. My stomach cramps up. Maybe that is why I am not hungry or thirsty. Maybe I am sick. Yes, that's it! I must be sick. I think I might throw up. I reach my right arm to my belly but I feel tremendous pain in my armpit when I move my arm. Doesn't matter. I throw up anyway. I don't care. I don't think I can care.

I close my eyes and talk to God. Lord, why is this happening? Why are you doing this to me? Please, Jesus, help me to remember that, in all my sufferings, I am united with you on the cross. Help me trust that my suffering is not in vain. Help me to know that you are ever close by my side. God, I offer up my despair and weakness to you. Please, give me strength and hope. Please protect me.

I open my eyes and I think I've been asleep. I see flies swirling around me. I lose them, though, as I am dizzy, spinning. It is hard to keep my eyes open. But I feel something strange along the seatbelt line, spots that hurt, from my hurt shoulder down to my right hip and across my pelvis. It doesn't feel like bruises, but like I have new cuts there, raw open wounds. I don't understand it. I look down and see new, red blood on my white shirt near a spot that hurts on my chest. My knees hurt, too, where they're pressed up against the front of the car. The skin on my knees feels raw.

I look at the grey mist through the blackberry bushes. I feel cold. I want to get warm. What can I do? Nothing, I guess. I close my eyes to shut out the spins but, in the darkness of my mind, the dizziness continues. I moan. At least, I think I moan. I am not sure.

From pitch black to pre-dawn, Tom stood at the end of the street, watching and waiting for Tanya. *Where could she be?* He *knew* that she was coming home but he didn't know when and he feared that, if he nodded off, he'd miss her arrival. He hadn't slept in three days.

As Monday morning came, he was listless. He staggered to his truck and drove to work on autopilot, and then he sat in his truck, listening to a sad song, over and over, waiting for seven o'clock.

He tried Tanya's number again. This time, it didn't ring. It went straight to messaging and, in that sickening moment, Tom realized that Tanya's phone had died. He began to sob and his whole body shook as if he was having a seizure. He couldn't move. He felt as if part of him died, as terror that ripped at him bubbled through his tears. He couldn't handle it. His thoughts descended to primal fear and dread and it was more than he could bear.

My eyes pop open. Here it comes again. I dread it. The nausea swells up like a wave but my body has nothing left. It doesn't matter. It comes anyway, in violent dry heaves that make my broken body cramp and lurch against the restraints. Shaking and locking down on my injuries and on all the other unknown processes that are taking place inside my body, my abdomen seizes and thrusts and spasms as I retch again and again, producing nothing. Please, God, make it stop, I say inside my head. Please, God, make it stop. Finally, it does, and I drift away.

"Lord," he prayed, "if you can't keep her safe, then keep her with you."

Finally, Tom gathered himself and sucked in a deep breath. He wiped his face and stared into space. *Maybe the detective has news*, he thought. He wanted to check in. He steeled himself and then dialed.

The detective asked if Tanya knew anyone in Yakima.

"No," Tom said, feeling a faint flash of hope. "Why?" In that instant, he thought he heard Tanya's voice calling him. *Was it wishful thinking? Maybe Tanya heard her phone ringing?* He realized that his tired mind was playing tricks on him. Her phone was dead.

"We had a tip on a car like hers," the detective offered. "In the parking lot of the Yakima Fred Meyers."

Tom felt hopeful. It hurt a lot less to think that, maybe, she *had* just left. Then, she'd be happy, at least. That was all he'd ever wanted for her—just to be happy. The news sparked a bit of energy in Tom as he worked on his chores. Still, he couldn't shake that nagging feeling—the screaming dread. It wouldn't go away, no matter what logic came his way. The despair tugged at his reasoning and barraged his mind with images of horror and the possibility of Tanya's death.

Tom thought about the detective's information for a while, and then he called her back. He asked her *why* she thought it was Tanya's vehicle. The detective explained that, in the morning, one of the Riders' credit cards was used there to buy gas.

Tom's heart sank. *He* had purchased the gas that day.

Why was the detective monitoring the wrong account? Tom wondered, confused. Tanya didn't have that card so he asked the detective why they were bothering to monitor it. The detective claimed that Tom had said that he didn't have access to that joint checking account. Tom felt weak, sinking. *Where did she ever get the idea that he didn't have access to their joint checking account?* he thought. Sarcasm riddled his voice as he apologized for whatever he might have said that had confused the detective. Again, he said, the *only* card Tanya had with her was her Nordstrom Visa. *All* of the other cards were at home. Nonetheless, the detective blamed the confusion on Tom.

The last thing he wanted to do was to slow down the cops, so Tom pent up his feelings about the detective. He knew well that, if he behaved badly, it would have slowed the effort to locate Tanya.

The detective asked him to print out his bank statements and, again, he explained that he had not yet set up his password. He feared that the police weren't really listening to him—or paying attention to Tanya's case at all.

Someone is looking at me. Through the dark nothingness, the night is eerily quiet, but I feel someone out in the blackberry bushes. Something is there, I can tell. The distinct feeling will not let go. I hear it! An animal snorts and I hear a crunch of the shrubbery. I freeze. I see a dark image move slowly, tentatively just outside the windshield. Oh, God! What is it? The rotten-egg smell permeates the night air and I have no way to clean myself and get rid of it, as I have always done with anything and everything in my life that was not clean, and I realize that the creature is not just attracted to the bushes but to the rotting-carcass smells imprisoned within my vehicle. The dark shadow grows closer, larger. Suddenly I can see the glint of an eye as the furry body sniffs back and forth. "Help!" I scream. "Get away from me!" Everything in my body hurts as I flail my right arm and try to bang on the console, the dashboard, the windshield. The bulk of the creature fades away. What was it? Oh, God, I'm scared. Please, God, deliver me from this darkness...

Tom felt restless. Too many feelings of hate, dread and grief welled up inside him. It turned the flavor of every food to ash. Though it was late at night and he was exhausted, he couldn't sleep. Tom stepped outside and walked down the street. His head rang with thoughts of vengeance when he thought about whoever had harmed Tanya. His vision focused on a blank face, its features absent. Tom was consumed with the need to know: What had happened to his wife?

I open my eyes and see a butterfly dancing on a blackberry bush somewhere near me. It flits around and in and out, here and there. I try to watch it because I like it. I think it comes inside my room and I raise my fingers toward it, but it flutters away. I look at my hand, and see that my fingers are puffy and swollen. Have I gotten fat? I don't care. My cheek itches. I would like to scratch my cheek but I don't bother. Instead, I close my eyes again so I don't have to look at the world spinning by me.

With my eyes closed, I think about swallowing but something tells me I shouldn't even try. But I think about my mouth. I have a weird taste in my mouth that makes me think maybe I licked some foil or a metal pan. I think that's crazy. "Strange," I said, maybe aloud. I think maybe I did actually say it because I smell something new, something very foul. I feel embarrassed. I think maybe it's my breath that stinks so badly.

Sometimes, I still feel my heart flutter so I think I am still alive. But I am tired—so tired. It is easier to keep my eyes closed and just rest. I can't even move, but I am so afraid of the animals, the darkness, the noises. I have been here for a long time. So long. I don't have any idea. Maybe it has been a few hours. It may even have been a few days. I don't know anything.

I talk to God. I tell God that I am sorry for anything bad I might

have done, but I can't really remember things like that right now. I tell
God that I hope I see Tom again, so I can tell him I love him. "God," I
say inside my head, "I do really love Tom, you know." God tells me He
knows.

It had been another short, fitful sleep and, yet again, Tom woke
with a start, his body drenched in sweat. Then, the sickening reality sunk
in: Tanya was still missing. The cops were still pointing their fingers at
him instead of aggressively searching for her. *Why?* He thought. *Why*
didn't they understand that he had nothing to do with her disappearance?
Worse, even, than that, the officials didn't seem to *care*, and the more
noise Tom made about finding Tanya, the more the police insisted that she
had the *right* to leave—to go wherever she wanted, whenever she wanted.
He had no say in any of it.

Was she gone forever? Had she left of her own accord, as the cops
insisted? The questions twisted in his mind as he tried to ready himself
for yet another day of more and more unanswered questions. Forced by
the situation, Tom had no choice but to let the days drag into one long,
sleepless miserable void, where unwelcomed and unstoppable thoughts
tormented him.

Hours and days overlapped, merging into each other. Tom's mind
was a blur, his life a painful swirl of time that held no hope. Each moment
of uncertainty was a waking nightmare, a slow-motion eternity. And Tom,
without Tanya, felt he had no reason to get through another day.

The police needed to act. And Tom needed to *make* them. He
distributed flyers and did everything he could, but he knew he needed to
keep the case in the news. After dealing with the police, he knew that, as
soon as they could, they would shelve the investigation. So, to keep the
pressure on and to force the police to search for Tanya, Tom offered a
$25,000 reward.

My breathing is rapid, each breath shallow. I am exercising. I am on my elliptical trainer, getting a workout. It feels good. Run, run, run. I like to feel my endorphins hit my bloodstream and then everything feels so good. I feel a drip of sweat on my face, just above my lip, and I open my eyes. I raise my hand to wipe it away. I look at my hand and see that it is fresh blood. I am not on my elliptical. I am in my grave. I raise my hand to my lip and feel for the wetness. I find it, below my nose. I look at my hand again and see that it is blood. I sniffle and taste it. I have a bloody nose? What the heck? I don't get bloody noses! I try to lean my head up and pinch my nose to make it stop, but I don't care. I'm tired. I want to rest. I need sleep.

I am at peace. I see the bramble of bushes surrounding me and I smell the ugly smell, but I hear birds and other sweet sounds. I am happy as I talk to God. He is with me, in my forest meadow. God knows who I am, and I tell Him whatever is on my mind. It is beautiful.

I think I was scared and hungry and thirsty but that was before. Now, I am not afraid, or hungry or thirsty. Now, everything is okay. I feel good. Life is good. Everything is so good!

Nothing hurts. I know I have had pain in my past, but not anymore. I have all I need in life. I have Tom. Where is Tom? Tom, where are you? Are you coming? Yes, I know you are coming! You'll be here. I know you will.

I drift off to a beautiful meadow, where the sun is shining. It's warm. Yes, it's warm! I see Lady, running over the grass. She runs toward me. The grass is dotted with wildflowers of every color imaginable. But it smells bad here. Why does it smell bad here?

I want to open my eyes, but they flutter. Can I open them? I see the place. Things are broken and dirty, disgusting. I want to get out, but I don't want to move.

At eight o'clock Thursday morning, Tom was on autopilot. He went through the motions of working. Every fiber of his body ached from lack of sleep as he drove to his first stop. He was in Tacoma when a King County Police detective called to request another "routine" interview. Tom had no problem answering more questions. "Where and when?" he asked.

They wanted him to come to the Regional Justice Center in the town of Kent, just south of Seattle. Tom called his boss, to let him know what was happening, and then it seemed to take forever for him to drive through sluggish traffic to Kent.

He struggled with his gut feeling that Tanya was fighting to get back to him—and to life in general—but he could feel her slipping away. Maybe he was just suffering from the effects of excessive anxiety and sleep deprivation, but reality started to grab at his heart and mind. He questioned his own feelings. Was there any hope of finding her? Would she be a different person if and when she came back? Was Tanya indeed fighting to survive? Nearing the Regional Justice Center, he let out an exhausted sigh.

He met the detectives in the Center and one of them asked if he was willing to undergo a polygraph exam. Tom readily agreed. First, they wanted to ask some "routine" questions of their own. They sat around a conference table with the tape recorder running while they went through their battery of questions. Then, they led Tom down a hallway to a small room. *Finally*, he thought. *Finally, they'll see for themselves that I'm in no way responsible for Tanya's disappearance!*

Since Tanya went missing, Tom's perception had slipped into slow motion and each second became an unbearable lifetime of strained and stretched moments. His lack of sleep showed on his strained face. Each step was a concentrated effort and each breath a labor. In such moments, Tom would have sworn that he could hear Tanya's voice talking to him, calming him, telling him not to do something stupid. "I will be home soon," her sweet voice said, "and then we can talk."

Those passing thoughts sustained him. Sometimes, he felt as if they were all that kept him from slipping over the edge where he would be swallowed in a very dark place. *Stay strong*, he reminded himself. *I'm the only one who can help Tanya, so I need to stay strong.*

Walking down the hallway, Tom's legs felt rubbery. With each step, he grew wearier. Passing faces in the hall, he noticed their sympathetic smiles, betrayed by looks of persecution in their eyes. He could see that they already had their answers. They assumed that he was guilty.

The polygraph examiner introduced himself and explained the procedure. Though his eyes were open, Tom had mentally dozed off into a dreamlike state.

"Tom," said the examiner, "I'm going to ask you a series of questions to make sure that we get a clean test. To get a clean test, there can be no surprises to taint your responses. Do you understand?"

"Sure," Tom responded. He didn't really care how the contraption worked or why, just wanted it to prove his innocence. Tom looked into the man's eyes and saw his disgust, as plain as if he had a sign tattooed on his forehead that said, YOU'RE GUILTY AND I'M GOING TO PROVE IT TO THE WORLD. Given the entire feel of it, Tom felt as if he was being led to the gallows, as if the wires would be woven into a noose to fit Tom's neck.

Finally, the examiner spoke. "Okay," he muttered, like a robot. "We can get started."

Tom could hear and feel the rhythmic beating of his heart and the wild turbulence of his sleep deprived mind, but the room was heavy with silence. He looked at the examiner.

"First question," he said. "When was the last time you saw your wife?"

Consumed with stress, Tom felt as if his body was pretty much shot. He wondered how his body would react to the strain of the questions, though Tom never hesitated with his answers. "It was Wednesday," he said. "In the morning before I took off for work. Tanya had the day off or, maybe, I should say the night off. She was still home when I left for work about five-thirty in the morning."

The examiner droned on about the upcoming question as Tom's mind continued to toss around his turbulent thoughts. *Oh, God!* his mind screamed in silence. *Where is she?* He prayed again, the same prayer he'd been praying for the past eight days: *Lord if you can't keep her safe, then keep her with you. Let no harm take her from you. Let no wrong be done to her. Keep her in your grace.* Again, the prayer sustained him, providing feelings of hope and peace.

"When you last saw your wife was she alright?" the examiner asked.

Tom felt a surge of anger, realizing that the police seemed far more interested in *him* than in his missing person—their victim. Tom looked at the examiner and sensed that the man expected the answer to be a lie. It must have been hard for him to understand that someone like Tanya could love someone like Tom. *Of course, he couldn't comprehend it,* Tom thought. *I haven't even figured it out myself!*

Tom never let his gaze leave the examiner's eyes and he never became nervous before answering. "Yes," he stated with confidence. He didn't even have to think.

At one-forty-five that afternoon, a search-and-rescue crew on case number 07-284-580 drove to the Maple Valley area of Renton to look for a cell tower in the neighborhood of State Route 169 and Jones Road. This intersection just happened to be on Tanya's route home from work.

"Our latest information would be a three-to-five-mile range southeast of the towers," the dispatcher told the rescue crew, Guardian One.

"Did you do anything to make her angry?" the examiner continued.

"No," Tom said. He tried to think of anything he might have done that rubbed her the wrong way but he came up empty. "I don't know," he said, expanding on his answer. "She's been angry at me about half the time we've been married and we've been together for a long time." He knew they wanted a yes or a no answer but the truth was that this was a grey area.

The examiner continued to ask the same question in several different ways, so Tom braced himself for the next variation on the theme.

"The last time you saw Tanya was she unharmed?"

"Yes," Tom answered.

"Have you ever hit your wife Tanya Rider?"

"*What?*" he seethed. "*No!*" He answered with a hint of attitude in his voice. Tom lost his patience and finally looked straight at the examiner. "Are these questions designed to make me angry while she's out there in God knows what condition?" he asked. "I think this is ridiculous."

"Easy, Tom" the examiner responded. "You have nothing to fear. Don't look at all the wires."

But Tom thought that it was next to impossible to ignore the mass of wires. He squirmed, although he'd done nothing wrong. The wires scared him.

"Ah, let's continue here, Tom," said the examiner. "We're almost done, I promise."

Tom doubted it.

"Did you do anything to hurt Tanya the last time you saw her?"

Before Tom could take a deep breath and answer the question, the examiner stood and stretched awkwardly.

"Let's take a break," he suggested. "I am going to let you unwind for a few minutes before we continue. Do you have any particular questions about the equipment?"

The only question on Tom's mind was, "Where's my wife?" But Tom didn't ask. Instead, he summoned all of his strength and simply said,

"No, I don't have any questions about the equipment or the test."

The search-and-rescue crew reported, "We have found the vehicle about a quarter mile south of the south end of Jones Road." In a moment, they added, "We have movement."

"Copy?" responded the dispatcher.

"We've got movement," they repeated.

The dispatcher then asked the County to send an aid car, saying, "It's that missing female, Tanya Rider, that was on the news. We found her vehicle and she's still moving inside of it! Whew! Wow! Goodness!" The dispatcher continued delivering instructions. "Just tell them to go really fast to the Jones Road off of State Route 169. Whew, got my blood pumping!" she added.

After giving directions for a moment, the dispatcher said, "Oh, my God. This is a car accident!" And, again, the dispatcher adds, "So this is basically, I think, a car accident and she's been trapped for this long! Wow! Where's the supervisor? Melinda? This is basically gonna be a car accident and she's been trapped in the vehicle ever since. Copy. Wow!"

The dispatcher turned to the rescue crew. "And this is just a blue Honda Element?" she asked.

"Yes, ma'am," came the reply. In a moment, the rescue crew added, "She's moving. That's all he told me."

The dispatcher canceled the car response as fire and medical personnel headed to the site and Guardian One, the helicopter, hovered above the scene.

The examiner left the room so Tom looked around to check out his surroundings. The small office was bare, with no windows and empty, white walls. Aside from the examiner's polygraph certification and a few other notices of achievements, the room had no decorations of any kind. The computer sat on an undersized desk and the various wires ran to a square case that opened like a suitcase. The box had several leads for various attachments—heart rate, pulse, blood pressure, and body temperature. Together, Tom thought that all the leads resembled spaghetti. He wondered how they could get an accurate test when the stress alone would make a person sweat? With nothing to do besides look around the boring room, Tom almost dozed off even though he was sitting erect in an uncomfortable chair.

Barely three minutes after the examiner had left, the door swung open. Tom recognized the detective, who had asked him for his computer several days earlier. Flanked by another detective and a uniformed officer, the detective came in, dangling a piece of paper from one hand.

What was going on? Tom wondered. *Why is it three against one?* Tom noticed that the paper held a map, but he could barely make it out through the fog that was overtaking his mind. Finally, he could see that the area on the map was a stretch of road he'd driven often—probably a hundred times in the past week. Tom was confused. He couldn't think of much that was there, along that stretch of highway, except the river and a stoplight.

Tom wondered what the map had to do with Tanya, and why wasn't the detective saying anything? He just stood there, looking at Tom. *Games,* Tom thought. *That's all they're doing—playing mental anguish games with me.*

The detective looked intently at Tom. Finally, he abruptly asked, "Do you know what a cell-phone 'ping' is Tom?" The guy didn't wait for Tom to answer. He showed Tom the map, which had a circle drawn on it. He pointed at it and explained that the last calls on Tanya's cell phone had gone through the same tower. In fact, every call attempted in the last eight days had gone through one single tower. They concentrated on Tom's reaction.

Time slowed down. Seconds turned into hours. Tom felt pure

dread.

The detective paused.

Tom was tired of waiting. "*And?*" he said, inching beyond irritated. *What are you waiting for? Tom thought. Why are you stalling? They're afraid to tell me!* His rage rose to the surface.

"We found her car," said the detective, pausing again.

Tom's heart rate surged into overdrive and his brain jumped into high gear. He had hundreds of questions. His head spun and a cold lump rose in his throat. It was hard to speak. He swallowed convulsively, trying to be calm, trying to finish his thoughts.

I open my eyes. What? What am I seeing?

I am scared. I look up at the passenger side of the car and I see a man's face. I don't know who he is. I am startled, scared. Why is he asking me so many questions? He is saying something but I cannot make sense of it. What is he talking about?

"It's a car accident," he says. "Oh, my God, it's her!"

Is he real? Or is my mind playing games with me again? Who is he? I do not think I know him. Where did he come from? Maybe he can help me.

I see that he's a police officer. He pulls open the passenger door.

Other people are with him. They are smiling and seem happy that they found me. I think I am happy, too.

"She's still alive," someone says.

"It's been—what? Eight days?" I hear another voice.

"She's still alive! We have to move fast and get her out of here. Oh, my God, I can't believe she's still alive!"

"Can you help me?" I asked.

I look at the man and his jaw drops. He seems stunned. He scrambles around.

"Do you have any water?" I ask. Then, they ask me questions and

I answer them, and I try to be friendly. I make them laugh. They work to get me out of my car, but I'm stuck. My car is smashed around me and they can't get me out. The fire department uses the Jaws of Life to cut apart my SUV. My beautiful, wonderful car.

"I can't feel my legs," I tell the medics. I am so tired I don't even want to breathe anymore. I close my eyes.

"I can't get a pulse," I hear somebody say. "She coded!"

CHAPTER TWO

Recovery

Tom couldn't stand it. "*And?*" he repeated. He had a flurry of questions: Where had they found her car? Had it been stolen? Did it provide any clues to her whereabouts?

"We found her car," the detective repeated. Then, he added, "In a ravine."

Tom didn't understand. He just looked at the detective.

"Are you familiar with 196th and Jones Road?"

Tom was very familiar with it, as he'd traveled that section of road many times. *Just come out with it!* he thought.

"She's still trapped inside."

Frantic, Tom's mind raced. It didn't make sense. *Why was the detective being so vague? What about Tanya? Is she alive?*

Tom held the wall to steady himself. "Is she alright?" he asked with a lump in his throat. He held his breath and studied the detective's face. *For God's sake, just tell me!* he thought.

"We don't know," he finally offered. "They're still trying to reach her."

Tom wondered what could have happened for them to be missing that information. His adrenaline and basic instincts threatened to overwhelm him with impatience, rage and fear, and he struggled to hold himself in check. He wanted a simple answer: Was Tanya dead or alive?

"Where are they taking her?" he stammered. "Which hospital?"

"Valley General," said the detective. "Do you want a ride?"

"No," Tom said, picturing himself in the back of a patrol car. "I'll get there on my own." Tom didn't want to surrender to the situation. He wanted to feel that he had at least a little bit of control so he definitely wanted to drive himself. He pushed past the three officers and ran down the hallway and out through the sky bridge to the parking garage. Disoriented, it took him a few minutes to find his truck. Finally, he jumped in, turned the key and merged into a nonstop line of cars in the midst of the lunch rush. While they went about the routine of their daily lives, he felt isolated in his own world of life-or-death panic.

He crept through the gridlock toward the freeway and entered Highway 167, northbound, heading for Valley General Hospital. His personal cell phone rang and Tom answered. A friend from work, Adam, told him that he was being detoured around the 196th and Jones Road area. "Something big is going on over here," Adam said.

"They found her!" Tom said. "They found her, but no one's telling me anything. The cop took forever to give me the little info he had."

"Did they find her on 169?" Adam asked.

"Yeah."

"I'm being detoured around her at Jones Road!"

"Can you see anything?"

"No," Adam said. "They're turning everyone toward Issaquah."

Tom's work phone rang. He answered the second phone and a reporter wanted to know if he had any comment on the fact that they were airlifting Tanya. His mind reeled. Valley General didn't have a heliport. That hospital didn't take airlifts.

"They don't airlift to Valley," he said to the reporter.

"No," she said. "Airlifts go to Harborview, I think."

"Can you see anything from where you are?"

"It looks like her car is face down in the water."

"*What?*" he asked in a panic. "She's in the *river?*" Clutching the phone, his fist squeezed around it until he heard something snap inside the phone.

"No, no," the reporter said. "She's on the other side of the road, in some sort of storm runoff ditch."

Tom had already passed the exit to Valley General so he said goodbye to the reporter and scrambled to change highways, finding himself in heavy traffic again. The cars eased forward as Tom searched the skies for any sign of the airlift chopper. Then he realized that he didn't know how to get to Harborview Hospital. He dialed 411, got the hospital's phone number, and asked the operator to connect him. In a panic, he talked himself through the directions. Finally, he found the hospital's neighborhood. He rounded the corner and saw a crowd of news vans parked in the bus and ambulance parking areas.

Tom circled down through the garage, searching for a parking spot. Five levels underground, he found a space. He shoved the cell phones in separate pockets, rushed to the elevator and punched the button. In a frenzy, he couldn't wait. He took the stairs two at a time. His work phone rang as he emerged at ground level. Adam asked if he needed anything but, just then, the reporters and camera crews raced toward him, blurting out questions.

"Adam," he said, "I'm low on smokes. And I'm being trampled by news crews. I'll talk to you later." Hanging up, he turned to the reporters. "I don't know," he offered. "I'm going to try to see my wife."

Tom found his way to the Emergency Room admissions clerk and asked about his wife. "Her name is Tanya Rider," he said, as calmly as he could. "She was brought in by helicopter from Maple Valley."

"I have no patient by that name," the nurse said.

"She's being airlifted," he explained. "This is where she would come, right?" Without waiting for an answer, he thought out loud, "Why isn't she here?"

Someone tapped him on the shoulder. Tom turned and looked at a woman, without really seeing her.

"My name's Susan," she said. "I'm the patient media rep."

Tom finally understood. Susan explained that she would help him to face the media. She was very calm, which unnerved Tom at first but, in time, her measured responses eased his stress.

"She's not here yet," Tom said, frantically. "How is it that she's not here yet?" Had he actually *beaten* the helicopter to the hospital? Though he had rushed through traffic, he figured that the helicopter should have landed before he got there. From what he could gather, Tanya had been transported to the local golf course for the airlift.

Tom paced a while before a nurse took him to a family waiting room, then he went outside to smoke the last cigarette he had on him. He was desperate for answers and his head was still spinning, but he realized that Tanya must have been alive—or clinging to life—if they were airlifting her. He returned to the family waiting room and Adam called again.

"I can see the chopper coming in!" he said.

Tom could hear the thumping blades of the chopper approaching the hospital. His heartbeat quickened. He would see his wife again!

"Thanks, man!" Tom said. Relieved, he tried to bolt through the door.

Susan intercepted him. "You can't go that way" she said in her characteristically calm voice. "And you won't be able to see her until after she goes through triage."

Adam arrived and Tom started to relax. He and Adam walked back to the waiting room but it took another smoke plus ten minutes before the staff gave him permission to see Tanya briefly. Arriving at the triage area, Tom and Nancy, Tanya's mother, found the floor littered with wrappers from the medical materials. He could tell that the emergency crew had done a lot in a short time, but it was evident that they had much more to do.

When Tanya's eyes found Tom, they softened and tears welled up in them. As the medical team wheeled Tanya past them, Tom saw the gash on her forehead, where a flap of skin was bunched up and scabbed in place. The medical team took his wife and disappeared around the corner. Tom looked at the x-ray hanging on the lighted board and saw a clean break of her collarbone.

Tom and Adam walked into a busy hive of news people who came from all directions with about six cameras and a dozen microphones pointed at him. Spilling out of their news vans, the cameramen stumbled over each other to keep up with the reporters.

"Mr. Rider!" they called. "Mr. Rider, do you have a comment?"

"My wife is alive," he said. "But barely."

Rushing to stabilize Tanya, doctors in the Harborview Emergency Room completed blood tests, x-rays and CAT scans. Since she was dehydrated, they intensively infused fluid near her heart. Her body temperature had dropped from the normal 98.6 to only 87.6 degrees, so they aggressively rewarmed her body. Her blood work revealed that she had too much sodium and acid in her blood. Further, her muscles had begun breaking down, releasing muscle fiber contents into the blood, which contributed to kidney damage. She was in acute kidney failure. Her lungs had leaked and she had air behind the abdominal cavity lining, in the middle of her chest, and in her right armpit. Her left shoulder was dislocated and she had fractures of her ribs, left clavicle and a spinal vertebra. A deep laceration on the left side of her forehead cut through her eyebrow, exposing the connective tissue sheath that covers the bone. From her seat belt, she had pressure ulcers on her pelvis, legs and abdomen, and deep patches of dead skin dotted her chest, abdomen, left elbow, both hips and both legs. And neither of her legs had a pulse.

Not only had Tanya been trapped in her vehicle, but her body was crushed. Her bones were broken and her lungs were leaking while she wasted away without food or water for eight days.

The Emergency Room transferred Tanya directly to the Intensive Care Unit, so Tom went up to the ICU waiting area. He was in a good spot to see Tanya as they wheeled her past him. She looked peaceful and beautiful, though she had an oxygen bag over her face and wasn't breathing on her own. Allowing the medical personnel room to work, Tom stayed back, but it pained him to be so close to her and, yet, unable to touch her. Desperate to help, he couldn't.

Finally, the doctor gathered Tom and Nancy, Tanya's mother, into a private conference room, where he talked about Tanya's condition in general and her left leg in particular. The muscles, nerves and blood vessels in Tanya's leg had been compressed for so long that the leg had developed 'compartment syndrome.'

The doctor said they had two options—removing the leg or trying to save it by performing a fasciotomy. This surgery had only a twenty percent success rate. If it did not succeed, Tanya—who ate only health foods and exercised faithfully every day—would lose her leg. While the doctor was trying to finish his explanation, Tanya's mother jumped up. "Take it!" Nancy screamed. Several times, Tom had to ask Nancy to quiet down so he could get all the information from the doctor, so that he could make an informed decision. Tom knew that Tanya would want to save her leg so that she could exercise, and the doctor said that it would not risk Tanya's life to try to save it. For Tom, this was the determining factor. He knew that, if there was even the smallest chance of success, Tanya's love of working out would win in the end and she would make it work. He made the call to save Tanya's leg. The medical staff rushed Tanya to the Operating Room for the emergency surgery, in which doctors relieved the pressure by cutting away the connective tissue covering her muscles.

In the waiting area, Tom's two phones rang nonstop. The missed calls and messages piled up. Late in the evening, Susan told Tom that the media were requesting an interview and she offered to set up meetings with the press, which Tom agreed to do so he could get it over with. Susan would need a few hours to set it all up.

To reduce the amount of shock on Tanya's body, the doctors put her into a medically induced coma. When Tom saw her after the operation, she was on a respirator. Longing to hear her voice, Tom watched her sleep. Her pulse was steady but she looked so frail, so thin. Her face was drawn and taut. Above her left eye, her forehead was bandaged, but he still thought she looked beautiful. Someone had braided her long blonde hair and coiled it into a bun to keep it out of the way, but dirt and blood still infused the matted mass and Tom found himself picking bits of glass from Tanya's hair. Her fingertips and knuckles were scabbed black. She had large bandages covering her torso, right thigh and her left leg, from her hip to her ankle. Tom sat silently watching her chest rise and fall to the rhythm of the machine that forced oxygen into her airways.

The nurses came back to check on Tanya and change her wound dressings. As the nurses moved Tanya, her moans tore at Tom's heart. To get out of the way, he left the room and wandered away for a while. When he returned, he sat and watched her for about an hour. Except for his prayers, his mind was empty.

At about three in the morning, it was time for Tom to face the news crews that had set up individual areas as their sets. The lobby was a mess of wires, lights, cameras and clamoring reporters, all wanting to break the story and all asking the same question: "What happened?" But only Tanya could answer that question. Susan directed Tom to sets for *Good Morning America, TODAY* and then others—the next and the next. Finally, he gave a press conference to answer questions from all of the local news crews. In each interview, Tom complained about the red tape but praised the Sheriff's office.

A news crew got him a hotel room, where he went for a shower, and then he checked on Tanya, who lingered in the deliberate coma. Tom came and went, looking in on her, sitting with her, hanging out in the ICU waiting room, and wandering around the hospital before he returned to sit by her side.

In the mid-afternoon, he found his way back to Tanya, who was still on the respirator. Her chest rose and fell and her eyes danced under their lids. Tom smiled, hoping she was having a nice dream. Looking at her, Tom considered the irony of what had happened. Before the accident, he and Tanya had finally been happy. For the first time, Tanya had seemed to be elated, finally living the life she had deserved to have from the start. Both of them had been in a great mood. Working for what they wanted, they chased the American dream and felt as if their lives were in perfect order—financially, physically and emotionally. Leaving all of their family turmoil in the past, they had moved on, made a clean break from Tanya's family a few years earlier, so the endless drama of Tanya's mother competing for her grandmother's favor had been stripped away. It had been liberating, like dropping dead weight. Indeed, everything had felt so right. And, then, in an instant, it all came crashing down.

The nurses returned to the room. They needed to move Tanya and, when they did, she cried out with tortured sounds, even though she was in a coma. While the nurses worked on Tanya, Tom wandered away to roam around the hospital for a while. When he returned, the nurse told him that they'd just removed the respirator. They had tried to do so earlier, but she hadn't been strong enough to breathe on her own. "This time," the nurse said, "she's doing just fine."

Tom went to her and saw that her color was returning. Taking slow, deep breaths, she looked like a sleeping, peaceful angel. A halo of golden hair surrounded her face, and Tom realized that someone had washed out the blood and redone her braids, although it was still very tangled. He also noticed that he finally smelled Tanya's familiar scent, not the sick smell of blood.

Tanya's doctor came in.

"How is she?" Tom asked.

"Well, she's breathing on her own and her kidneys are back to one-hundred percent," said the doctor. "All in all, she's doing much better than we could have hoped." The doctor smiled with confidence at Tom. "We're going to keep her unconscious for another day or so, to give her body more time to heal."

Tom looked down at Tanya and noticed a slight smile across her lips. Wherever she was, Tom knew that it was pleasant. After the doctor left the room, the nurses came in to change her dressings again. After enduring the regimen for a few days already, he knew that the entire procedure took the nurses about three hours. He left the room.

Tom avoided the news crews and walked with his friend Jonathan out to his car. Jonathan worked for SoundBuilt, the small company that tom worked for. Jonathan told Tom that Gary, their boss, was going to pay Tom for his time off and that he didn't have to return to work until Tanya was ready. Tom's coworkers at SoundBuilt offered to give Tom their vacation time and help with the house. Jonathan also offered Tom his condo near the hospital, so Tom could shower, change and rest when he needed to, and then he took him to the mall to pick up some clothes. SoundBuilt paid the bill, and then Jonathan treated Tom to a hefty steak for lunch.

When Tom wandered back to the hospital, he found a cart full of flowers and a growing stack of cards and letters from around the world. While Tanya slept in the coma, Tom read some of the letters to her, believing that she could hear his voice at some level.

The doctor returned with more good news. They would keep her in the coma for a while longer, but her kidneys continued to function at one-hundred percent. Her leg was still in jeopardy but it, too, was slowly improving. As the hours passed, and days turned into night, Tom continued to meander through the hospital hallways whenever the nurses came in to change Tanya's dressings. He'd eat an energy bar or gulp down a cup of coffee or a 5-Hour Energy shot, and then he'd return to sit by Tanya's side. Refusing to sleep until Tanya was out of danger, Tom picked up more of the cards and read them out loud to her.

My most powerful first memory was seeing Tom. Stronger than anything, clearer than the pain of those first days, the image of his face is the first thing I remember. They had me so loaded on medication that I wasn't sure any of it was real, but the first thing that I knew was real was Tom. He was standing over my bed, smiling at me.

Another time, I woke up and realized that there were lots of people around me, fiddling around my legs. I asked the nurse for something to drink.

"We have juice," she said.

I was disoriented. I had no comprehension of the seriousness of my situation, so I looked at her and asked, "Does it have sugar in it?"

"We have water," the nurse replied.

"Bottled?" I asked innocently.

The nurse stared at me, incredulous. She couldn't believe that I'd be so picky.

Then, another nurse tried to get me to tell her what had happened. "Do you remember going off the road?" she pressed me. "Did you fall asleep?"

I didn't even know who was asking me the questions. Though I had asked for my glasses, no one could find them and I couldn't see past the edge of my bed. This added to my fears, as I couldn't even clearly see the faces of the people around me.

"I don't know," was all I could tell her.

When Tom returned to Tanya's room, her mental fog had lifted. She was coming out of the coma and he was elated. But, then, Tanya spoke.

"Why did you leave me down there for so long?" she asked, scowling at him with pure hatred in her eyes.

Tom had never heard her speak in such a cold, hateful tone. He looked at Tanya and felt crushed by the look of pure loathing on her face.

Tom noticed that Nancy was soaking up all the turmoil and she seemed to be enjoying the look of pain on Tom's face. He looked at Nancy. Tom realized that Tanya's mother had been in the room, talking to Tanya, before Tom walked in and he couldn't help but wonder if Nancy had put the thoughts into Tanya's head.

"I called you for help," she added. "I even called the police and they laughed at me!"

Tom couldn't bear it. He was stunned, and felt the blood drain from his face. Heartbroken, he didn't know what to say or do, and he couldn't bear the look on her face or the tone in her voice. His mind reeled. He turned and left the room.

Walking down the hospital corridor, he latched on to something she had said. *Had she really called 911?* Shaking with anger, he fumbled through his stack of business cards, found the detective's number and left a voice mail. Then he called the radio shows to vent his anger. He wanted to use the media to get the message out that what had happened to Tanya should never happen to anyone. He wanted to honor her survival by making sure that such disasters didn't happen to other people. He wanted to tell the world that 911 operators need to be trained to handle missing-person reports with understanding, compassion and urgency, and that police departments need to establish more effective criteria to safeguard human lives.

After Tom's rant, the Sheriff called one of the local radio shows, trying to curb the damage to her department. Then, the Sheriff called a press conference. Although she hid behind "procedure," she did apologize to Tom for the "poor customer service" he'd received from those who served under her command. That was worth something, Tom thought, feeling vindicated that, at least, he had made the Sheriff see why the system needed to change. But it wasn't enough. And, as soon as Tanya was found, it seemed to Tom like the games began. Tom thought the Sheriff's office acted like a small child playing a game of "Look over there! Don't look at us!"

Tom walked into my room and I gave him the best smile I could manage.

"What happened?" I asked. "Why am I in the hospital?"

"You were in a car accident," he explained.

"How's my car?" I wanted to know. "Is my Element okay?" It was the first new car I had ever gotten and I loved it! Tom told me not to worry about anything but getting better. Then, he said something that confused me.

"Babe, you're a miracle," he said.

"What? A miracle?" I asked. I didn't understand how I could be a miracle. "Why?"

I tried to get him to tell me what he was talking about, but he wouldn't. "Not yet," he said. "Just concentrate on getting better so you can get out of here..."

"I don't understand," I persisted.

"You were lost for awhile and then we found you," he said. "That's enough for now. Don't worry. You'll have your car when you're ready and we have all the time in the world. Just get better and I'll take care of everything else." I could tell by the look in his eyes that I would not get any more answers, so I let it drop for the moment.

I was heavily medicated for the next few days and my mind and memories were blurry but I know that over and over and again and again, I asked Tom about what had happened. I wanted the full story but he kept telling me to just worry about getting better. Then, a few times, he said more, but he stopped when he sensed that I couldn't handle any more. He was right. I couldn't handle much at first. "We'll stop there, for now," he told me. "Just know that you're loved." Still, sometimes, I'd forget and ask him again.

It took me a while but, the more I learned, the more I saw God's *hand in it. How else could I explain it? To live for eight days is well beyond the odds. I believe that He kept me safe and, mostly, whole. For the most part, I still have all my parts. Some are changed, some are banged up, and most have new scars, but—even with the scars—they're still mine.*

The lead surgeon entered the room with an entourage of nurses and medical students.

"We have to get her ready for surgery," said an older charge nurse. "So, you'll have to come back later."

Although he had only been able to spend a few minutes with Tanya, Tom felt revitalized. He was grateful that they had Tanya so doped up that she wasn't in as much pain and didn't seem to remember what had happened. When he came back, he brought Tanya her cell phone, which she kept under her pillow so that she could call him whenever she needed to.

Meanwhile, some good Samaritans had gone to the accident site and searched for things that had been left in the ravine. Among other things, they found Tanya's social security card, a book that contained the plans for the house she and Tom were building, and other important papers. The person had retrieved the items and returned them to Tanya with a note that said, "I thought you may need these." As a true act of kindness, this gift was given to Tanya with no claim for credit. This good Samaritan gave part of Tanya's dream back to her, without even leaving his or her name.

Each day, Tom told Tanya a little bit more about her ordeal. He stopped when he thought it was too much for her.

When the hospital moved me from Intensive Care to a regular room, I asked them not to give out any information about me without my permission, including my room number. Tom was the only person I wanted with me and the only person who was to know where I was. But, in the confusion of the shift change, the staff almost wouldn't tell Tom where I was. Tom was about to cause quite a scene when the nurse I had talked with happened to walk by, on her way out for the night. "This is the husband," she told the others. "He's the only one who is to know where Tanya's new room is."

Twice a day, the nurses needed to change the dressings on the wound on my left hip. To do this, they had to roll me over and, in the process, they dug their bony fingers into me. While they were trying to help me, I don't think they realized how much pain this inflicted on me so, finally, I refused to let them roll me. Instead, I asked Tom to help me. His strong, fleshy hands and gentle touch didn't hurt, so he was the only one who could roll me onto my side without pain. In fact, this routine gave me an unexplained comfort. Unlike the nurses, who were in a hurry to go help other patients, Tom took his time working with me and getting me into position, and then the nurses could access my wounded hip, change its packing, and change my other bandages.

I couldn't stand to watch. While a nurse changed my dressings, I asked for a washcloth and put it over my eyes but, when Tom was there, I'd look into his eyes, where I saw his love. It made me feel safe because I knew that, no matter what, he would be with me. We got married in 1998 and, like most married couples, we fight—and I win—but Tom was always there to support me. Of all the crutches I could lean on, Tom was the most comfortable. Plus, he could always make me laugh and bring out my joy—even in the hospital.

Although I was under the constant mask of pain medication, most of the time I could still feel the pain and it was almost too much to bear. Through it all I drew strength from Tom. He was there, always there. And he was sure I would walk again, even when I was not.

The doctors and nurses told me that I needed to get up and move around. I listened to them, and I heard their words, but I couldn't imagine how I could possibly do it. How could I get up and get around when I was still in so much pain? How could I regain my strength when the constant diet of painkillers left me even weaker? I'd been in the hospital for about a week and, so far, I hadn't been able to move much of anything. Even the simplest tasks were beyond me. Movements that used to be so easy, so simple, would cause me so much pain.

After hanging from my seatbelt and trapped in my car for eight days, I suffered nerve damage to my left arm and ankle, leaving them useless. It was as if they were dead. I was unable to control even the simplest movement in either of them. Due to the nerve damage, I had no mobility in the fingers in my left hand and my left wrist flopped down. I was powerless to lift it back up. For my wrist, I had two different braces—one for sleeping and one with springs to hold my fingers straight.

I'd had surgery to close the deep laceration above my eye and another surgery to repair my left collarbone, which had been broken clean in half. It was still healing from the surgery and I wore a sling to immobilize my left arm, which the doctor told me not to move. It seemed as if all of my pain was concentrated at the center of my body, while the edges of my body—my sides—felt dead and numb, as if dosed with Novocain. I had several muscles—including three on my left hip—that had died and the doctor had to carve the muscles out of me, all the way down to the bone. After the fasciotomy, I had three more surgeries on my leg. Then, every two days, the doctor came to remove the wound-vac tape from my leg. The pain from this procedure was worse than anything I had ever felt and, at this point, that is saying something!

Several hoses tethered me down. In addition to the wound-vac hoses, I had a catheter as well as IVs that drowned me with a steady diet of medication. They forced much of this medication on me and it caused such nausea that I had no appetite, so then they added two anti-nausea medications to my growing list of pills and shots. It seemed as if they monitored my blood with blood draws every two hours, leaving me with only short naps in between. This was a hell of its own. Locked and alone in my car for eight days, I wished for someone to come. But, imprisoned in a hospital bed, I just wished for some time alone so I could rest.

Those weeks were a blur of pain medication and, through it all, I felt powerless and trapped. My caregivers told me what to take and when, and they would not even allow me to take my own vitamins. For someone as health conscious as I am, this was traumatizing to me. I felt even more powerless than I had in the car. Unable to move or to use my damaged, medicated mind, I was at the mercy of nurses. And, although the care I received in the hospital was exceptional, not all of the nurses were nice. Some of them, it seemed, didn't like their jobs. They let it show. But I almost have to thank those nurses. More than anything, their attitudes and their way of doing things convinced me to take back control of my life. Before long, I wanted up and out. And, when I want something, I make it happen. It took about a week of trying and sweating and failing. With hard work and a lot of determination, I would take back my life.

Even as doped up as I was, I tried to sit up. I don't remember how I did it, but I did, and then I felt like I was going to throw up and I was sure I was going to die. Still, I had a beautiful view of Seattle and, for that moment, I could see that people were still living their lives out there. It hit me that I wasn't living my life. I wasn't being productive. I wanted to get better so I could get back to my life. In this moment of clarity, I knew that I would do it. I would walk again. I realized that Tom was right—as usual—but I'm not going to tell him that!

"No matter what," I told Tom, "do not allow me to quit!" I made him make a pact with me and he stuck to it. He was there, always there, and I drew strength from him. As long as he was there to shadow me and assist me, I felt safe. I knew that Tom wouldn't be distracted and he would never let me fall. He wouldn't get paged away at just the wrong moment, as the physical therapist had. The stability of knowing he would be there helped me cope with the reality that my life had become.

We took it step by step. My first project was just to sit up but even this simple task was a great challenge for me. The first time I tried it, with

Tom's help, I broke out in a cold sweat. Dizzy, I couldn't continue. My muscles had been torn in the crash and, throughout my ordeal, they had lost even more strength, so I was extremely weak. But I had to keep working on it. It was the only way for me to improve my condition. If I didn't push through the pain, no one else could do it for me. I always recognized that, no matter what the circumstances, there are just some things in life that we have to do for ourselves. Each time I tried to sit up, the effort made me break into a sweat, but I was determined! More than anything else, I needed to regain control of my life and the first step would be to retrain my body—to let my body know that my mind was in control.

Of course, the pain was excruciating. Even through the constant mask of medications, the pain was almost unbearable most of the time. But, when I complained about my leg pain, Tom reminded me that it was okay, because feeling the pain meant that the nerves weren't dead and I still had my leg. He was sure that I would walk again.

Sometimes, he was relentless in asking me to do more—and I hated him for it. I know, I asked him to push me, but did he have to be so good at it? When he pressed me, I could see the longing in his eyes and I suddenly realized how hard the whole ordeal must have been on him. Still, sometimes, I got to the point where I just wanted to yell, "No!" at him. That's when he'd find a way to make me laugh. He could always make me laugh.

It worked. Soon, I was able to sit up and, by the end of the next day, I could almost sit up without help. It's strange to be so proud of accomplishing such a simple thing! By the third day, he asked me to repeat each motion more than once. "Can you do that once more for me?" he'd say, continuing to push me.

I always tried hard but, some days, I only succeeded with help from Tom. Being so close to him, I found great comfort in his scent but, when I looked at him, I realized that he was unkempt. Putting all his effort into my recovery and devoting every waking moment to my needs, he was not taking care of himself. The evidence was plain on his furry face.

Before long, I could sit up by myself, so then we set a new goal—sitting on the edge of the bed. The first time, I almost passed out because the pain was beyond anything I'd ever felt before and it scared me. Then, after a short rest, Tom gave me a generous helping of encouragement and asked me to try again, so I would. And, no matter how small my progress, Tom's eyes lit up and made me to want to do more.

But I began to wonder if this would be our lives from then, on—me, trapped in a bed, with Tom chained to my side, not letting me give up. As I improved, I drew strength from the look of pride in his eyes and, before long, I didn't want to let him down. When the doctor came in and saw me sitting on the edge of my hospital bed with Tom hovering nearby, a look of utter amazement flashed across the doctor's face. It was more incentive for me to push myself.

I had told Tom what I needed from him and he focused all his energy into making it happen. Almost a month after the accident, Tom and I started to work on standing. I thought I was going to die. For a moment, I was sorry I hadn't. The pain was excruciating. I cried, straining over each movement with my teeth clenched to build my strength. But, almost an hour into that session, I stood by my bed as Tom supported me. One of my nurses did a double take as she walked by my room. She nearly tripped. On my third attempt, he asked me to go again. I started to notice that, the nearer I got to total collapse, the more I could do the next time.

The next morning, Tom helped me stand and sit five times. Each session, he prodded me. "You can do more," he'd say. I admit that, sometimes, I'd flash him a nasty look or balk at his suggestions, but he always reminded me that we'd made a deal and he was just keeping up his end of the bargain. As we went on, he would decrease the amount of support he gave me and, at the end of each session, he'd go and get me a reward for all my hard work. Since I suffer with depression, a therapist once told me that I needed to do things to make myself happy—which should be my number one goal. When Tom brought me small rewards for working so hard, it helped, making me feel productive again. Jamba Juice smoothies—with an energy boost—were becoming my favorite as I went from sitting up to standing.

I could hardly believe the look on Tom's face the first time I stood up all by myself, and I got such a kick out of the nurses who walked past my room. Their heads whipped back in disbelief at the great progress I'd made in the hours since their last shift. One time, a crowd gathered to watch and I sucked all the strength I could from their wide eyed looks. As Tom steadied my walker, I stood for a few seconds before I sat back on the edge of my bed, and then I repeated the motion.

After that, we worked on taking my first steps since the accident. Threatening to give out, my legs were rubbery and protesting with pain like I had never felt before. But, as soon as I recovered, I was standing in front of the mirror, brushing my teeth and looking in the face of a stranger. Knotted in a swirl, my untidy hair stood straight up in the air. "This isn't me," I kept telling myself as I looked at the image of the stranger in the mirror.

Soon, I was getting out of bed and brushing my teeth without any assistance. I know that most people think that brushing teeth is such an easy task. Yes, most people take it for granted but, of course, I was not like most people. Before they give it a shot, they should try strapping on about five-hundred pounds and then try to brush their teeth. I think that might approximate what such a simple task was like for me, with the weakness in my legs and the missing group of muscles in my hip.

One time, I almost went down. I was showing off for Tom by trying to take a sideways step. It seemed simple at the time but I suddenly felt as if I'd been shot by a Taser. I was in so much pain! Tom flew across the room and caught me before I fell.

Day after day, we worked together. Finally, I could sit and stand without much assistance. Whenever we completed a certain number of repetitions, we'd move on to something more demanding. Though every movement was slow, tiring and grueling, I kept my mind on my goal and Tom gradually pulled back, withdrawing his support so I had to rely on my own body more and more. With my mind coming back to normal and, finally, in self-control, I was determined to force my damaged body to regain control, as well. As much as I wanted my mind and body to be back on the same page, it was as if they were fighting a civil war, and both were determined to be the victor. The whole time, neither my body nor my mind would freely give an inch so, finally, I determined that I would have to join the battle and fight against two enemies.

The next phase of my workouts involved getting in and out of my wheelchair. I was always very cautious, but I had a good sense of my body and knew what I was capable of, so I never fell. My skill at getting into my chair improved and, finally, one day, Tom and I went for a push around the hospital. My tangled mass of hair stood straight up at the back of my head, but Tom still looked at me as if I was the most beautiful woman in the world. I could tell that he was proud of me, too, for all the work I was doing. That motivated me even more.

But, then, Tom had to go back to work. He worked all day and then came to see me in the evenings, bringing my dinner and some food for the next day. Then he went home to shower and sleep before going back to work again.

On his first night away, Tom called to tell me that it looked like some "confused burglars" had broken into our house. He said that, instead of stealing anything, these bungling burglars had left some things—a kitchen set, washer and dryer, bedroom set, tables and lamps. All of these things had come from Tom's boss, Gary, who pulled the furniture from some of his model homes. He'd also had a fence built, made the first six payments on our mortgage, and paid Tom for the time he was at the hospital with me. Through everything, Gary had been there for us. Thanks to him, I would be able to return to a comfortable home—and have a bed to sleep in.

But being alone most of the day was a setback for me. Without Tom there to push me, I had to push myself. It was very scary for me. Even though I was getting stronger, I felt more vulnerable because Tom wasn't there to catch me. And I missed him. But all of these feelings steeled my resolve to be home by Christmas. To do that I had to prove myself to the rehab team, and I had to pass all their tests. I had to! I had made up my mind and, now, all I had to do was convince my body.

Unaware of the extensive media coverage about her case, Tanya watched a DVD that Tom brought to the hospital. The DVD recapped some of the media coverage, including Tom's appearances on media outlets. Though Tanya said it was incredibly sad, she also felt that it was incredible. Her story of survival reinforced her belief in the amazing power of God and she strongly believed that God played a part in her survival and recovery. She felt blessed.

Still, Tanya had a hard time. She still had no control over her left ankle, which drooped, getting in the way when she tried to take steps. Finally, the therapists made her a brace to keep her foot from dropping. It was an improvement, but walking was still a great challenge. "Many times, I almost fell backwards," she said. "It was really traumatic to realize I didn't have control of my body." That was all she wanted—control over her own body and her own life.

After she was at Harborview for about a month, her care team noted that she was emotional and crying, so they asked the psychiatry team to evaluate Tanya for anxiety and depression. One of the physical therapists had pressured Tanya to stand and walk from her chair to her walker, without holding on to anything. Afraid that she would fall, Tanya felt that the therapist was pushing her too hard, so she refused to do it. In response, the physical therapist threatened to transfer Tanya to a nursing home if she didn't try harder. Anxious about falling, Tanya refused to do it and refused to work with that therapist again. Dreading a bleak future in a nursing home, she had cried after the altercation with the therapist.

Despite all of her operations, Tanya was able to stand and transfer into a wheelchair with little help, just two months into her recovery. From lying down to sitting up and from climbing out of bed to sitting in her wheelchair, Tanya worked as hard as she had every worked at the gym before her accident. "It was like the two-hour workout I used to do at the gym," she said, "just getting to the bed or to the potty." And then, already past the point of exhaustion, she still had to get all the way *back* to her bed.

As the weeks went by, the therapists needed to decide whether Tanya would transfer to a more accelerated inpatient rehabilitation unit or to a skilled nursing facility. They would prescribe the nursing home option if they felt she wasn't expected to make much progress. But, to qualify for inpatient rehabilitation, Tanya had to reach certain milestones and complete many tasks. For example, she had to be able to sit up for a period of time and perform a certain number of exercise repetitions with her hands and feet. Determined to spend her first Christmas with Tom in their new home, Tanya wanted to do her best at passing *any* tests the doctors put before her. At every turn, Tanya worked hard to challenge herself and to surpass their expectations.

But it was difficult. Having lost so much fat and muscle, she was thin and prone to bedsores, which exacerbated her pain when she sat still. Her workouts made her dizzy. And though she fought anxiety, fear and frustration, she did not want to be a victim. "I *had* to get out of the wheelchair," Tanya said, "and up to the walker!"

Though her body was suffering, Tanya still refused to surrender to it, refused to give in or give up. Tom continued to press her, asking for "just one more try," and Tanya complied, even when she didn't feel like it. Starting with a walker, she took baby steps. Tom followed, pushing the wheelchair close behind Tanya so she could sit when she got tired. She took short rests to take a long pull from her water bottle and then she'd be up and off again, pushing her walker down the corridor. At first, the hospital hallway looked immense and her first trip down the hall was painstaking and tedious. But, soon, they were making trips around the therapy wing and Tanya found that, the more she pushed herself to her limit, the better the next day would start.

Before her accident, Tanya had been committed to a healthy and disciplined lifestyle of vigorous daily exercise and a nutritious, natural diet, so she had a hard time with the hospital's food service. To help solve the problem, Tanya enlisted the support of a hospital nutritionist, who helped to arrange for the kitchen to provide Tanya with healthier alternatives. And, each evening, Tom brought dinner to Tanya along with a nice supply of organic foods that she could eat whenever she wanted. Until this time, Tom spent every night in Tanya's hospital room. But, then, Tom's friend couldn't watch the dog anymore and, since it was cold out, Tom went home to let the dog into the house.

After Tanya had been in the rehab wing for about two weeks, the rehab team challenged Tanya with a "real life" test. They gave her ten dollars and a bus ride to Whole Foods Market in downtown Seattle, and required Tanya to buy food for one meal, pay for the groceries, and make it back to the bus. Tom didn't want to miss the excursion. "I think he needed to see me get out," Tanya said, "even more than I needed to *be* out."

Tanya made it into the store. Walking down the long aisles in the store, she was aware that the distances she had to walk were far greater than the trips she had made around the hospital's hallway. To meet the care team's challenge, Tanya had to purchase a minimum of three ingredients that would make a balanced meal, but she could not spend more than ten dollars on her purchase. The test was as mental as it was physical.

Working her way down the first aisle, she collected one of the components for her meal, which was simple but filling and required at least five ingredients: eggs, brown rice, mayonnaise, lettuce and bread. She started to tire as she reached the next aisle. Tom disappeared. Though he wasn't allowed to help her shop, he found a way in which to help. He snagged a chair from the deli and brought it to her. Since the test had no time limit, it wasn't against the rules for Tanya to rest, and Tom could tell she needed it. But, being her determined self, Tanya wouldn't stop. Though her body wanted to give up, her mind refused to rest and, in the end, her mind won.

Tanya continued shopping as each step brought a greater wave of pain. She felt a little warmer than usual and then sweat formed along her hairline. Pushing through the sensations, she kept going, though she started to feel weak. By the time she finally had her stuff together, sweat trickled down her face and dripped from her chin. Grateful for a short rest, Tanya took a seat in the chair for a few minutes. Sitting there, waiting, she considered her own determination. *I'll show them what I'm made of,* she thought. *And I will make it home for Christmas!*

Recovered, Tanya headed for the check out register, where she stood at the end of a line of people. Finally, she paid for her food. Tanya was tired. It had been a demanding outing and she still had to get all the way back to the hospital. Finishing her transaction, she and Tom headed for the exit, but a large group of people who were milling around, just talking, blocked Tanya's path. Tom pressed into the small crowd and offered a few choice words that elicited some strange looks before the group quickly moved out of the way. Drenched in sweat by the time she finished her simple shopping errand, Tanya walked outside and the cold air hit her "like a knife."

Thinking about the pain she experienced on her simple shopping trip, Tanya wondered about the level of pain her body had suffered while she was trapped in the vehicle for those eight days and nights. Although she remembers some of the pain, her mind spares her from the vivid memories. It is as if the sensations became photographs, like memories that have become facts but with detachment from the emotional experience of them. The facts exist, but she doesn't *feel* them. In a way, Tanya feels this may be a blessing.

Having met the strenuous test, Tanya faced another challenge the next day. In this test, she had to *cook* the meal for which she had bought the ingredients. But, when she arrived in the kitchenette where she had stored her groceries, her ingredients were gone. Having endured all the pain and effort to shop for her own, healthy groceries, Tanya was horrified that someone had walked off with them. The rehab team reworked her test, challenging Tanya to make a meal using any ingredients in the kitchen. She did but, in the end, she was glad she didn't have to eat it! "I'm sure it was a fine meal," she said. "But it wasn't *my* food. It wasn't the food that I had chosen to cook and eat. It wasn't the meal I had fought so hard to get."

Tanya remained determined to prove her commitment and she made steady progress. Once she transferred to the unit, the rehab psychologists consulted with her and continued to note her anxiety and her tendency to "micro-manage" her therapy. Feeling fearful and vulnerable, she wanted *control,* but didn't have any. She was at the mercy of her damaged body. On the other hand, her appetite was increasing and her endurance improving.

At Tanya's first meeting with her care group, she and Tom held hands. The team asked Tanya her goals and she said, "I want to go home for Christmas." When they told Tanya not to get her hopes up, she broke down and cried. In early December, she had a second meeting with them. The caregivers asked her what her goals were. Tanya said she intended to be home for Christmas. "We'll see," they said, rolling their eyes. Tanya thought they seemed more than noncommittal—even a little shocked—as they again warned her not to get her hopes up. "They didn't know me," she said. "And they didn't know how determined I was." She took their equivocations as a challenge and, Tanya says, "I never back down from a challenge."

Before long, I graduated to a cane. Sometimes, I could even putter around my room without it, though, one time, Tom had to catch me. But, generally, my progress astounded my nurses and other onlookers on my floor. Partly, I did it for Tom—for the pride I saw in his eyes as he pushed me—but I also did it because I didn't want to be dependent on anyone or under their control. I was sick and tired of being told what to do. I wanted to go home.

When I entered the room for the third meeting with my care team, I walked in using just my cane. Their eyes popped and they looked at me as if I was wearing a jet pack! Again, they asked me what my goals were and, again, I said I would be going home by Christmas, which was only two-and-a-half weeks away. Still, they looked doubtful. As a group, they all seemed to say that I shouldn't set my hopes too high. I felt a little angry and defiant. I wanted to show them that I could do it.

The next day, I pushed myself to exhaustion—and then some. My body kept trying to fail but I refused to let it.

"Do you want to rest?" my therapist asked.

"No, not yet," I said. "I want to go a little farther."

She told me that I was pushing myself too hard but, before the accident, I ran six miles every morning, so I knew I had the strength in me.

"I'm okay," I said. "Just a little more, and then I'll rest."

After ten weeks in the hospital, I took another field trip, for fun. My head and hair had taken a beating and my hair hadn't been thoroughly washed or brushed for almost three months. It was a matted mess. Tom took me to a salon where they detangled my hair. It was a massive undertaking as two very patient young women worked for more than two hours, standing on each side of me and untangling my hair. I remember the pain of sitting in the salon chair for those two hours. Oh, God! I had no meat on my bones and, although I was sitting on a comfortable padded chair, I felt as if I was sitting on two jagged rocks and, sitting there for so long, I

*felt my bones pinching my skin. I tried to keep a stoic face and attitude but,
whenever I made the slightest move, the pain shot through my body.*

*By the time I had to leave to return to the hospital, the women
didn't finish. They had detangled the sides but didn't make it to the middle,
having detangled about half of my hair. I walked out of the salon sporting
a tangled half-Mohawk that stood straight up from the center of my scalp.
I don't know how he managed it, but Tom looked so proud, walking next to
that! And I felt good. It felt so good to have my hair mostly fixed and I felt
like things were looking up. Most of all, I was excited that I would soon
leave the hospital!*

Tom's heart was heavy. Despite his joy that Tanya was finally
coming home, he felt overwhelming dread.

He'd kept the reality of their financial situation to himself but,
soon, he'd have to tell Tanya. After all those years of working two jobs
so they could buy their land and build their home—after all the sacrifices
they'd made so they could achieve their dreams—they would probably lose
everything, *even the house.* After all they'd been through, after all *she'd*
been through, they would have to start over. The bills were mounting and
they already had more bills than they could pay. Collectors were calling
for payments. Tom and Tanya's dreams were slipping away.

Tom had to come up with eight-thousand dollars to make a down
payment to Harborview Hospital. To help Tanya recover, he would have
done whatever he had to do. He managed to raise the money but, then,
Tanya's insurance wouldn't pay for a portable wound vacuum for her
recovery at home. The wound vacuum creates negative pressure in a
wound, pulling blood to the surface, encouraging healing and promoting
scar tissue formation. Tanya had used one at Harborview Hospital but
couldn't continue this treatment at home, even though the device would
have sped up her healing time. Tanya was almost relieved, for nothing
compared to the pain of changing the tape on the wound vac. "None of the

other pain came close to it."

For her part, Tanya had made great progress during her three months in the hospital. She could stand up on her own and walk with a cane. She could navigate stairs—up and down—if someone was close by. And, more or less, she could dress herself. She was ready.

Tom bought Tanya a cute outfit for the big day. Tanya never allowed Tom to shop for himself—much less for her—because he usually chose extreme clothes in loud colors. But, when he gave Tanya her "going home" outfit, she was pleasantly surprised. He had picked out a pair of black bell bottom workout pants that had enough room to accommodate the brace that she wore on her foot, and a pretty shirt that was large enough to allow her to get her left arm into it. Tanya could tell that he put more than the usual amount of thought and effort into choosing the outfit. She was proud of him, and more than a little touched.

On December 21, 2007, Tanya was discharged from Harborview Hospital and Tom picked her up in Tanya's brand new, blue Honda Element—one year newer than the one in which she'd been trapped. Tom had asked her what kind of car she wanted and she'd said she wanted the same car. "He knows how hard it is for me to buy good things for myself," she said. "So, before I got home, he replaced my car." Just like its predecessor, the car was named "Skywalker."

Her discharge diagnoses included trauma with multiple wounds including open wounds on her hip, abdomen and thigh. She also had a shoulder dislocation, left wrist drop, left foot drop, deep-vein thrombosis, anxiety and depression. More than anything, she was in pain. Upon discharge, she took home twelve different medications, including an antidepressant and significant amounts of pain medication. Continuing with physical and occupational therapy, Tanya would also have to make doctor visits—endlessly—and she needed a visiting nurse.

They didn't go straight home. On the way, they stopped in at the salon again so the women could finish what they had started. They fixed the rest of Tanya's tangled hair. Tom and Tanya had planned to attend a Christmas party but, by the time they got home, she was shot. But she was home for Christmas!

As the car approached the house, Tanya smiled when she saw that Tom had made a snowwoman in their front yard. Walking into the house, Tanya first noticed the couch set that Tom had bought her for their anniversary. She made a straight line to the couch and sat down with a smile on her face. Then she looked around. Living alone in his "man cave," Tom had made a mess of the house. Tanya was too tired to express how mad she was, so she decided to save her anger for the next day. Besides, she realized the he still needed her as much as she needed him—not to clean up after him, but to make him do it. This thought comforted her and she barely got herself situated in her new bed before she drifted off to sleep.

Tanya found it much easier to rest at home compared to the hospital, where loud nurses, medication, and other intrusions might interrupt her sleep at any time of night. She was also free of bedpans, hospital smells, the lack of privacy, and the loss of control. But the cycle of sleep-pain-dressing change, sleep-pain-dressing change, sleep-pain-dressing change, which had droned on like a broken record throughout her hospital stay, was not over.

Tanya still had open wounds that needed twice daily cleansing and dressing changes. Early every morning, before he left for work, Tom woke Tanya and changed her dressings. It was hard for him. Some of Tanya's wounds were deep—to the bone—and Tom couldn't get used to looking into them. After awhile, though, this became a natural part of his routine and, in time, Tanya took charge of changing her own dressings.

A month later, when Tom took Tanya into the Rehab Clinic for an appointment, she was struggling. Although she was making steady progress *physically*—able to prepare her own light meals and walk around the house—she faced some emotional challenges, primarily with fear and anxiety. She couldn't drive, so Tom chauffeured her to wherever she needed to be but, whenever she got in the car, she was afraid of getting into an accident. She felt uncomfortable if he drove near other cars. And she suffered with disturbing dreams, nightmares and night sweats.

One of the high points in her recovery was the day the doctor cleared her for driving. She'd lost her driver's license in the clothing that the hospital had cut from her body, so she had to hassle with getting a new license, starting with providing proof of birth and citizenship. Once she obtained her license and the doctor's permission to drive, Tanya felt like she was back in the driver's seat—in more ways than one. The liberation of being able to drive was so important to her that Tanya added it to her list of things for which she was grateful.

Her injuries, especially the open wound on her left hip and right thigh, continued to require treatment and she could not go back to work yet. But, less than six months after her discharge from the hospital, Tanya could walk without her cane.

Despite her scars and her ongoing medical needs, she felt fortunate that Tom, the 'love of her life,' still found her attractive. Though she lost her engagement and wedding rings in the wreckage, she felt that the rings symbolized the love between Tom and herself, which, she believes, grew stronger through their ordeal. Tanya's faith in her marriage and in Tom's love helped her to let go of her concerns about her appearance. The only person she wanted to impress was Tom, and Tanya did not concern herself with what anyone else thought of her. Tom feels that Tanya can accomplish whatever she sets out to do, though it may take a lot of work. And, from a place of deep love for her husband, Tanya believes that all things are possible for her.

When I came home from the hospital, my first goal was to get off painkillers, but I'm still on them. Without painkillers, I am in constant pain from nerve damage as well as from my wounds. These wounds get infected and, recently, I had three infections in a row. They keep recurring.

Because of these chronic, non-healing wounds, I've been in and out of the hospital since my original discharge. And, though I returned to work at Nordstrom's as a customer service representative, I wasn't able to keep it up. I had to go on disability. But, always, I am grateful to be alive.

During the eight days I hung inside my car, pinned by the steering column and the door, I was unable to move anything but my right arm. My body had been crushed, wrapped in metal that held me until they rescued me. In the deep void of those eight days, I instinctively knew how to calm myself to survive the ordeal before me.

I continue to question why the police did not conduct an immediate search and, as a result of this questioning, I feel some loss of faith in law enforcement and some concerns about the limitations imposed by their procedures. The fact is that the police can't and don't always protect us. We need to protect ourselves. We need to be aware of our surroundings, to notice who comes and goes in our neighborhoods, and to be proactive about our safety.

Before I crashed into that ravine, I was in exceptionally good physical condition. Not long before the accident, I had asked Tom to purchase an elliptical trainer. He agreed, and I faithfully spent at least an hour on the elliptical trainer every day. This may have helped save my life and, so, I believe that I was fortunate. Even today, I enjoy working out on the elliptical, which seems to help me be more mobile for the rest of the day. And it lifts my spirits to know that, after all that has happened, I can still do it.

Trapped again in the hospital—in a non-functioning body—I was at the mercy of nurses, doctors, rehab therapists and other caregivers. I did what I could, but I was very limited. Still, I wanted my freedom. I wanted my life back. I fought for it and I won.

Looking at my ordeal against the backdrop of my life story and my battle with depression, I know that people wonder how I got through these years without sinking down into depression. To put it simply, when things are bad, I try to see the positive side of life because I believe that it is unproductive to look only at what is wrong, without also trying to see what is right.

People seem to want to see my scars but they are mine and mine alone. That is how it will always be. I work very hard to keep my scars a secret. I recall the pain and trauma as well as my strength and victory. I recall that, with prayer and my husband's love, I found the strength to survive my physical terror and my mental wounds. I made it. Tom made it. We are the proof that—with prayer, hope and love—we can survive anything. For that, I am so grateful.

CHAPTER THREE

Your Loved One is Missing

I was five years old and my brother was two. We were playing in our yard in Placentia, California, when a man tried to abduct us. My mother called the police, who came to our home. I gave as good a description as I could of the man.

Later that same year, Stephen came tumbling out of an orange grove about a mile from our house. Witnesses watched him cross a busy intersection while two young Boy Scouts were trying to catch up with him to make sure he was okay. We never knew whether Stephen wandered away from our house—and walked a mile to the orange grove—or if someone took him and dumped him among those trees.

I was too young to understand what any of these things meant. But my mother knew. And, of course, as I grew up and had children of my own, I came to understand all too well.

When a child goes missing, many parents feel that their worst nightmare has come true. And, whether your child, spouse, dear friend or another loved one is missing, it will not matter *why*, but that they *are*. You will likely feel hopeless, helpless and uncertain. You will probably not know what to do or what to expect and, like Tom Rider, you will probably bounce back and forth—over and over—between an urgent adrenaline rush and a sickening sense of powerlessness. Unable to eat, you will be weak with hunger and, unable to sleep, you will be drunk with fatigue. And you will probably find yourself afraid to leave the telephone and tending to gaze out the window or down the street, wishing that your loved one would just show up.

Despite the chaos of the emotions you will endure, you *will* get through it. And it is very important that you do because *you* will play an important role in solving the puzzle of finding your loved one. Your involvement can be key in bringing your loved one home.

When someone is missing from your life, it is a sad comfort to know that you are not alone. The National Center for Missing and Exploited Children (and Adults) (NCMEC) reports that, on average every year, 58,200 non-family abductions occur where a juvenile is held for longer than an hour. Forty percent are taken from a vehicle or from the street and 16 percent are taken from their home or yard. Approximately half are sexually assaulted and a third physically assaulted. In the vast majority of these cases—71 percent—the abductor was a stranger, and 21 percent of the time, the abductor was a slight acquaintance. Of the tens of thousands of children who are grabbed and held for at least an hour, less than one-fourth are reported to police. For several reasons, the rest of the cases go unreported. Many of those who are taken and released are afraid to tell their families or the authorities, since abductors often claim to know where families live and threaten to kill family members. Also, as a result of what the perpetrator did to them, some kidnap victims feel dirty and unworthy of rejoining their family so, often, they keep their ordeal a secret. Still others return to tell their families, who might discount the story and not believe what has taken place. As a result, just over twelve-thousand abductions are reported to law enforcement annually.

Several hundred-thousand juveniles and adults go missing every year. This encompasses all cases, from runaway reports to stranger abductions. The statistics are staggering and they are real, and they indicate that Americans are enduring an incredible loss of loved ones in greater numbers than ever before.

As a result, countless resources are available to help people search for their missing loved ones. Across the country, government entities, nonprofit organizations, and consultants advocate for improved systems that will help us prevent abductions and accidents and, when they do happen, provide help and support in the work to recover the missing. Police, state patrols, and federal agents have developed and constantly utilize ever-better tools for investigation, tracking, and publicity, and, at all levels—local, state, and national—we have more laws and more effective laws to help turn the tide of abductions.

Still, the system is not perfect. It failed Tanya and Tom Rider. In a country where hundreds of thousands of people go missing every year, each of us must consider that, one day, it could be *our* neighbor, *our* child's friend, or *our* loved one who slips through the cracks and disappears. Yes, it is alarming.

While none of us wants to live in constant fear or act paranoid, we *must* be diligent. It is important to be prepared and one of the best ways you can do that is to arm yourself with information. Take simple steps to avoid getting lost. Know what to do if you are in an accident, trapped in your car. Carry emergency supplies. And if the unthinkable happens and someone you love goes missing, know what to do. If you are caught in a situation like the one Tom Rider faced, you would have an important advantage if you are aware of a few essential facts. Be familiar with the laws that govern missing persons investigations. Know the truth about filing missing persons reports—to whom you should report, when to file a report and where to go for help, for example. And know your rights. Find out what you can do if the local police department claims that your loved one wasn't in their jurisdiction or if they refuse to file a report.

Efforts to Bring the Missing Home

I am a 911 dispatcher. Trying to make a difference, I teach law enforcement classes on active shooter incidents and crisis negotiations for the non-profit Association for Public-Safety Communications Officials, APCO International. I am also a volunteer instructor for NCMEC. As one of a handful of APCO adjunct instructors, I teach telecommunicators the best-practice protocol in handling child exploitation calls and incidents involving missing or abducted children and adults. The NCMEC sends me and other unpaid volunteers to travel across the country on our own time, doing everything we can to teach dispatchers how to give missing persons the best chance of returning to their loved ones.

I do this work because I want to answer the calls—and help others to answer the calls—that I could not make as a child and young adult. Growing up in a transient family, I had a secret: Despite appearances, my childhood was a disaster because my father was abusive. He remains in prison today as retribution for his crimes against me and many others.

To navigate the missing person system, it is important to be knowledgeable about how that system works, what is available, and how agencies interact and share information. At the national level, missing person reports are entered into a computerized database called the National Crime Information Center (NCIC). The NCIC began in 1967 and added missing persons records in 1975. NCIC has grown to include a variety of records and today, for example, it includes stolen property, people on the National Sex Offender Registry, known or suspected terrorists and more. The NCIC averages 7.5 million transactions per day and, by the end of 2009, it contained more than fifteen-million active records within nineteen files.

When a person is reported as missing, the information is entered into the NCIC. This information can include name, date of birth, height, weight, eye color, hair color, sex, race, social security number, scars, tattoos, a photograph, and the name and contact information for the case's investigators. NCIC retains each missing-person record until the individual is located or until the law enforcement agency that entered the record cancels it.

As of December 31, 2009, NCIC had *active* missing-person records on 96,192 individuals, more than half of whom were juveniles. During the 2009 calendar year, 719,558 missing persons were entered into NCIC; this was down from 778,161 entered in 2008. The NCIC classifies missing persons into six distinct categories of persons who:

- have a proven physical or mental disability (classified as Disability— EMD);
- are missing under circumstances indicating that they may be in physical danger (classified as Endangered—EME);
- are missing after a catastrophe (classified as Catastrophe Victim— EMV);
- are missing under circumstances indicating their disappearance may not have been voluntary (classified as Involuntary—EMI);
- are under the age of 21 and do not meet the above criteria (classified as Juvenile—EMJ);
- are 21 and older and who do not meet any of the above criteria but for whom there is a reasonable concern for their safety (classified as Other—EMO).

In 1999, the NCIC implemented an optional Missing Person Circumstances (MPC) field, which allows the law enforcement agency entering the data to code the missing person as Runaway, Abducted by Non-Custodial Parent or Abducted by Stranger.

Once local law enforcement enters the missing person data into NCIC, the information is accessible nationwide. During a search, any criminal justice agency or federal, state or local law enforcement agency can pull up the file, instantly. But, before acting on any information obtained in the NCIC, an inquiring agency must contact the agency that originally entered the report into the database to ensure that the information is accurate and up to date. After confirming the record, if the inquiring agency has made a match, they can return the missing person to their home. For persons who are not located, initiating law enforcement agencies are required to send a validation report to the NCIC annually, stating the cases that are still open. To keep the database pristine, the NCIC removes from the database any records that the originating agencies do not confirm or validate.

In some cases, the NCIC records do not include sufficient information to identify a person. In May 2005, to address this problem, the NCIC implemented another field in the missing person database, allowing law enforcement agencies to store, access and supplement dental records. The National Dental Image Repository (NDIR) field helps to facilitate the identification of missing, unidentified, and wanted persons.

Law enforcement can also file a report with the National Center for Missing & Exploited Children, which can assist with making and distributing wanted posters and age-enhancement technology, tracking, notifications and research. Families can also contact NCMEC on their hotline at 1-800-THE-LOST for help and support.

Another important tool at the national level is the National Missing and Unidentified Persons System (NamUs). Developed to help solve cases, NamUs is the first online repository for records on missing persons and unidentified persons. Accessible to the general public, NamUs provides access to coroner and medical examiner offices, and allows you to narrow search results by searching multiple characteristics, such as sex, race, dental information, and tattoos.

Suzanne's Law

Prior in 2003, law enforcement agencies were only required to report missing persons who were under the age of eighteen. As a result, countless numbers of missing people over the age of eighteen stayed missing and many of them still have not been found. One such person is Suzanne Lyall, a student at State University of New York at Albany. She has been missing since she exited a bus at Collins Circle on the University at Albany Uptown Campus on March 2, 1998. Police did not begin investigating until nearly two days after her disappearance and, as a result, her family has waited for answers for more than twelve years.

Suzanne's case inspired President George W. Bush to sign "Suzanne's Law," which requires police to notify the NCIC immediately when someone between the ages of eighteen and twenty-one is reported missing. Suzanne's Law also amended Section 3701 (a) of the Crime Control Act of 1990, eliminating twenty-four-hour waiting periods, which were common practice for most law enforcement agencies. Now, law enforcement agencies cannot enforce any waiting period before they begin an investigation of a missing person under the age of twenty-one.

In August 2008, President Bush took Suzanne's Law a step further, signing a bill entitled The Suzanne Lyall Campus Safety Act, which amended the Higher Education Opportunity Act and required colleges to have policies outlining roles for law enforcement agencies at the campus, local and state level in the event of a violent crime on campus. The Suzanne Lyall Campus Safety Act was designed to minimize delays and the confusion of roles in investigation.

In response to Suzanne Lyall's disappearance, New York also enacted its state's Campus Safety Act in 1999. This Act requires all colleges in New York to "have formal plans that provide for the investigation of missing students and violent felony offenses committed on campus."

Adam Walsh Act

On July 27, 2006, President George W. Bush signed another important piece of legislation, the Adam Walsh Child Protection and Safety Act of 2006. This Act was named after Adam Walsh, the six-year-old son of John Walsh, creator and host of *America's Most Wanted*. Adam disappeared while shopping with his mother, Reve Walsh, in July 1981. Two weeks later, after extensive searches, a fisherman found the boy's severed head in a Florida irrigation canal more than one-hundred miles from home.

Two years later, a drifter named Ottis Toole confessed to killing Adam Walsh. Though Toole told police that he and his lover—serial killer Henry Lee Lucas—abducted and killed Adam, the details didn't add up. Police began interrogating harder and learned that Lucas had an alibi: He had been in a Virginia jail on a car-theft charge and could not have been involved in the case. Faced with the evidence, Toole admitted that he had lied about Lucas's involvement and, finally, police had the kidnapper/murderer, and a confession. Toole even provided details of the case consistent with police findings and described a wooded area where he claimed to have left Adam's body. But police were unable to locate the child's remains and they had no physical evidence to validate the confession. The state attorney declined to prosecute the case. Toole subsequently changed his story and, three months later, he recanted his confession.

According to John Walsh and others, sadly, several lapses (including the loss of DNA evidence) marred the investigation. Though Toole twice confessed to killing Adam, he never served time for murdering the boy, though he served five life sentences for other murders. On his deathbed in 1996, he confessed to his niece that he was, indeed, the killer. In 2008, authorities finally announced that they had closed the case on Adam's murder after definitively determining that Toole had killed him.

Two years before authorities closed the case, John and Reve Walsh hoped to save countless other families from dealing with the horror they had endured. They set forth the Adam Walsh Child Protection and Safety Act of 2006, legislation that established a national sex offender registry and made significant changes to sexual abuse, exploitation and transportation crimes. The act also created new substantive crimes, expanded federal jurisdiction over existing crimes and increased statutory minimum and/or maximum sentences. As part of this program, the Act established a three-tier classification system for sex offenders:

- Tier III. The highest tier is "a felony sex offender convicted of aggravated sexual abuse or sexual abuse, or abusive sexual contact of minor under age thirteen; non-custodial kidnapping; or any sex offense committed after the person becomes a tier II offender."

- Tier II. This includes "a sex offender convicted of a felony charge or attempt to commit sex trafficking, coercion and enticement, transportation with intent to engage in criminal sexual activity, or abusive sexual contact; if it involves use of a minor in a sexual performance, solicitation of a minor to practice prostitution, or production or distribution of child porn; or any sex offense committed after a person is labeled a Tier I offender."

- Tier I. This covers any sex offender not classified under the second or third tier.

Depending upon the classification level, sex offenders must remain registered for a specific period of time, and it is a felony for a sex offender to fail to register. Tier I sex offenders have a registration requirement of fifteen years but they can appeal for reduction after five years or removal after ten years. Tier II registrants are required to register for twenty-five years, and Tier III offenders must register for life, though they can appeal for removal or reduction after twenty-five years.

National and State-based Alert Systems

The actions and options available to families and law enforcement are slightly different if the missing person is a child or an adult.

In cases of missing children, law enforcement agencies can issue an AMBER Alert if the case meets certain criteria. First, law enforcement must confirm that an abduction has happened and assess the level of risk to the child. If the child is abducted by a stranger, the level of risk is much greater than if the child was abducted by a family member. So, authorities can release an AMBER Alert if:

- a child is at risk for serious bodily harm or death;
- there is sufficient descriptive information on the missing child or possible abductor;
- and the child is seventeen years or younger.

In these cases, AMBER Alert data is immediately entered into the National Crime Information Center (NCIC) and the case is flagged as a Child Abduction. This expands the search from the local level to the state, regional or national level, increasing chances that the child will be located. A Child Abduction flag will also trigger an immediate response from the FBI and NCMEC, which will contribute resources to aid in locating the child.

For missing persons over the age of seventeen, other alert systems are available and, often, these vary by state. (This chapter includes resources in specific states.)

State of Washington Procedures

In the State of Washington, police will go into action if an adult is missing under certain circumstances. To activate an EMPA in Washington:

- the person must be missing under unexplained, involuntary, or suspicious circumstances;
- the person must be believed to be in danger because of age, health, mental or physical disability, in combination with environmental or weather conditions, or is believed to be unable to return to safety without assistance;
- law enforcement must be given enough descriptive information that could assist in the safe recovery of the missing person.

Once police *at the appropriate local jurisdiction* determine that the missing person meets these criteria, they will activate the action plan and prepare an Endangered Missing Person Advisory (EMPA) through a central computerized system. This notifies all Washington law enforcement agencies including the Washington State Patrol Missing Persons Unit (MPU). The local jurisdiction should follow up with the State Patrol's MPU to verify receipt of the EMPA. The MPU can issue the EMPA locally, regionally and statewide. The EMPA is also sent to the media and is entered into the NCIC database as well as a similar, state database, the Washington Crime Information Center (WACIC), which includes information on missing/unidentified person cases.

As soon as authorities obtain a photograph of the missing person and/or suspect, they add these into the databases and email them to the State Patrol's Missing Persons Unit. The MPU can then provide the investigating agency with electronic posters that include details of the missing person. If the missing person is twenty-one years of age or younger, the National Center for Missing and Exploited Children encourages the investigating agency to make contact with them.

The investigating law enforcement agency assigns a Public Information Officer (PIO) to handle press inquiries and provide updates to the media as much as possible. This is an important component. Missing-person cases rely on the media to garner maximum exposure, as this encourages the public to relay any leads to the investigating agency or dispatch center. When the investigating law enforcement agency receives new information, they then can update or cancel the EMPA, as appropriate.

In Washington, the State Patrol's Missing & Unidentified Persons Unit is also available to assist local law enforcement agencies in locating missing persons. The MUPU works with other state, national and international organizations to compare and share information on missing persons cases; it has a repository for dental records, DNA and human remains information so that they can match up any recovered, unidentified persons or their remains with missing-persons cases.

The State of Washington is also home to the Missing and Exploited Children Task Force, which assists local and state law enforcement agencies by conducting investigations relating to crimes against children.

Several national organizations also provide additional help at no charge to searchers. A Child is Missing, for example, uses an automated telephone system to contact local residents and businesses if a child, elderly or disabled person goes missing. Team Adam provides agencies with child abduction investigators, technical assistance and equipment during investigations that involve missing, abducted, or exploited children. Additionally, Project Alert offers the help of retired federal, state, and local law enforcement officers to assist in investigations of missing, abducted, or exploited children.

One major complication in missing persons cases in Washington and elsewhere is the lack of evidence pointing to where a person has gone, or—if they were abducted—evidence pointing to a specific suspect. This often leaves investigators with little information to go on. According to Washington law RCW 68.50.320, if a person is still missing thirty days after the initial report, the police *must* file a missing person report with the State Patrol's MUPU. DNA, therefore, should be collected from the missing person's belongings, as well as from their family members, so that law enforcement can conduct DNA testing. Law enforcement will also ask the family or next of kin to give written consent allowing officials to obtain dental records for comparison.

What Went Wrong in the Rider case?

The State of Washington in general and the Seattle area in particular have come under scrutiny for inattentive and even sloppy handling of missing persons cases for many years. In 2003, the *Seattle Post-Intelligencer* published a yearlong, ten-part exposé entitled "Without a Trace" by Lewis Kamb.[1] This series documented that Seattle-area police (as well as agencies around the nation) made frequent and costly errors in missing persons cases.

For example, when a child is reported missing, police enter a report into state and national databases in hopes of catching a break in the case. If, after thirty days, the child is still missing, the police are supposed to send medical and dental records to a state agency, which can use the records to identify a body in the future. According to the *Seattle Post-Intelligencer*, the State of Washington has about 2,100 missing-persons cases on file at any given time. About two-thirds of them, 1,400 cases, involve people who have been missing for thirty days or longer. But the *Post-Intelligencer* uncovered that the police had *never* followed up on nearly two-thirds of the 1,400 cases and the state and national files still did not include the medical and dental records of more than 900 missing persons.

Without this proper follow-up, several cases mistakenly remained open even after the missing person was found. But, worse, police

85

closed cases based on unconfirmed sightings or rumors of the person's whereabouts. This was the case with four women believed to be victims of the Green River Killer, who murdered forty-eight women in an area south of Seattle. Although the women had actually been dead at the time of the "sightings," police had closed their cases and, because of these costly errors, they lost valuable clues to the killer's identity.

According to the *Seattle Post-Intelligencer*, another problem with missing-persons investigations in the Seattle area was that, often, *the missing person was never reported missing*, possibly due to inconsistencies in report filings. "Some departments would accept only those reports filed by a family member; others would take them from friends or associates," the article reported. "Some departments had a waiting period—three days in some cases—before they'd take a report. Some refused to take a report if the person lived or disappeared outside their jurisdiction."

These are precisely the issues that precluded Tom Rider from convincing the police to open a case on Tanya—and, unfortunately, these issues are not unique to Seattle or Washington!

Consider a situation in which you realize that you haven't heard from your Uncle Joe in a while. You call him and he doesn't answer. His answering machine is full. You stop by his house and his mailbox is overflowing. You call his office and they say that one day, about two weeks ago, he just didn't show up and they haven't seen him since. Should the police take a report and open a case so they can find your uncle for you?

First, we have to consider whether this is an appropriate use of our police resources. Also, consider the possibility that Uncle Joe might not *want* you to find him. What if he went through a humiliating breakup with his girlfriend and went to Hawaii to mope for a while? What if he is on a bender and doesn't want his relatives to know that he drinks? What if he has any one of a million secrets and all he wants to do is to go away to keep them private? Should our police departments help you find him, just because you don't know what he's been up to?

The fact is that every American adult has the right to privacy—even your spouse, sibling, parent or best friend. Children do not have the right to go missing, but we adults *may* choose to ignore our friends, leave our jobs, set our sights on a new destination and disappear into the sunset, never to be heard from again. We can do this on a whim and we do not have to ask permission or even tell anyone. *Any adult can be voluntarily missing* and many people *really do* want to disappear on purpose. It is not a crime and these people are entitled to their privacy. Even if police investigate such cases, they may not be able to divulge information about that person unless or until the person gives them permission to do so.

In some cases, "missing persons" have also been victims, survivors, and/or witnesses of previous crimes. Each state establishes its own rights and programs for people who have been involved in criminal or juvenile court proceedings. The federal Witness Protection Program, for example, is full of people who are missing because *they do not want to be found.*

If suspicious circumstances surround a person's disappearance or it is out of character that the person can't be found, the law enforcement agency in the jurisdiction where the person was last seen must decide whether the situation meets *their* qualifications. If it does, they will file a missing persons report. However, in the State of Washington, the local jurisdiction will make this decision on a case-by-case basis, and it is a grey area—not black and white. Therefore, when loved ones call the police in Washington about a missing adult, the police will first want to determine—by their own, subjective measures—if the person is missing against their will. Until they determine this, law enforcement will limit their involvement. This subjectivity slowed the investigation into Tanya Rider's disappearance.

The issue is whether such determinations should be subjective. The answer is no. *All* police jurisdictions throughout the United States should follow the NCIC's model. In terms of missing persons, the NCIC system covers:

- A person *of any age* who is missing and who is under proven physical/ mental disability or is senile, thereby subjecting that person or others to personal and immediate danger;
- A person of any age who is missing under circumstances indicating that the disappearance was not voluntary;
- A person of any age who is missing under circumstances indicating that that person's physical safety may be in danger;
- A person of any age who is missing after a catastrophe;
- A person who is missing and declared unemancipated as defined by the laws of the person's state of residence and does not meet any of the entry criteria set forth above.

The FBI's criteria are similar. The FBI will consider an adult's disappearance a missing person incident and open a missing person file if the case involves:

- Disability (physical or mental limitations);
- Endangered person;
- Involuntary disappearance;
- Juvenile (a person under 21);
- Catastrophe Victim (missing after a catastrophe).

In situations that meet one of these conditions, the FBI declares the person missing and opens a record. However, when the missing person is over the age of twenty-one, the FBI requires that documentation be signed in order to protect the individual's right to privacy.

By any such standards, the police in the Rider case should have filed a missing person report and initiated an investigation immediately. The circumstances of Tanya's situation obviously indicated that her disappearance was not voluntary and that her safety, therefore, may have been in danger.

Furthermore, the Bellevue police told Tom that, since Tanya drove away from her night job at the Fred Meyer store, she had left their jurisdiction. They told him to return home and call his local police department. This was incorrect. According to Washington law, the correct jurisdiction is the local police department *where the person was last seen*. Rather than passing the buck to the King Country Police Department, the Bellevue police should have taken the report and investigated the case.

Further, since Tanya was a reliable worker who never missed her job without calling, and she suddenly missed several shifts in a row, her disappearance was clearly unexplained and suspicious. Given that she did not take money, left checks at home and only carried one credit card, her disappearance did not appear to be voluntary. Tom argued—rightly—that Tanya must have been unable to return to safety and that she must have been in danger. Still, the local police initially refused to investigate. By the time they did, it was almost too late. Tanya Rider suffered and almost lost her life as the direct result of law enforcement failing to ping her cell phone sooner.

What to Do If Someone You Love Is Missing

Your loved one is missing. What do you do?

First, remain calm. Panic will only hinder your ability to think straight.

The immediate question is whether to call the police right away or wait. Many people believe that you must wait twenty-four or even seventy-two hours before you can file a missing persons report. *This is not true! There is no required waiting period needed before filing a missing person's report!* It is never too soon to contact the police if:

- someone witnessed an abduction or you have reason to believe that someone took your loved one;
- you know of suspicious circumstances;

- the missing person is a child or an adult under twenty-one years of age;
- the person is over the age of sixty-five;
- the person suffers from physical or mental illness;
- the person has been depressed or suffers from depression;
- the disappearance is out of character.

If someone witnessed an abduction or other suspicious circumstances, or you have reason to believe that someone took your loved one, call 911 immediately.

In 2002, the Department of Justice completed a long term study looking at 880 cases of children who were kidnapped and murdered. This study found that 47 percent of these child victims were killed within the first hour. Within three hours, 71 percent are gone. Within twenty-four hours, we are down to a 9 percent survival rate. The first hour is what we call the "Golden Hour." It is our best chance to recover an abducted child alive and, for this reason, when a child—or any loved one—goes missing, it is absolutely critical that you act swiftly and decisively.

To report that a person is missing, call 911 or visit a police station. You will need to describe the circumstances of the disappearance, with information about the last location where the person was seen. The police will also ask you to provide medical information, if any, for the missing person.

If you know that your child or another loved one has been abducted, *do NOT call their cell phone!* As long as that phone has power and is turned on, we have a chance to track it. If the phone rings and an abductor hears it and becomes aware of the phone, they will take it and turn it off and then the phone will no longer be of help.

Search

If your loved one is a child, start at the last place where you know that someone saw them. If your child is missing from a store or location outside of your home, immediately notify the store manager or security office as well as the local law enforcement agency. If your child is missing from home, you should thoroughly search the house. Check closets, in and under beds, inside large appliances, inside vehicles, the garage, attic, and any other place where your child could hide. If you do not find your child, contact the local law enforcement agency.

If your missing loved one is not a child, you first need to determine whether you have sufficient reason to believe that they are missing. Look everywhere that you can possibly think of. If you cannot find them, contact friends and family and ask if they have any idea where the person may be, if they have heard from them, or if they know of anyone else who might know where the person is. Enlist help in contacting more friends and family so you can focus your energy on other tasks. Anyone who makes these calls should keep track of everyone they talk to, recording the name, phone number, and time of the contact. Someone should stay by the phone at the missing person's house at all times, in case the person calls or returns home.

If you search for the person and cannot find them, contact local law enforcement officials and file a missing persons report. Some jurisdictions will not classify a missing adult as a missing person.

In the case of Tanya Rider, each time Tom called 911, the dispatcher gave him a different homework assignment—to call the hospitals, to check and see if Tanya was in jail, and to call her family. Police will handle your case much more efficiently if you make these calls *before* you try to file a missing person report. Of course, if you have a witness or any reasonable evidence that your loved one was a victim of foul play, you should call 911 immediately. Otherwise, you *do* have an obligation to look for the person, and this includes contacting family, friends and the local jails. (Normally, a hospital would have notified you if your loved one was in an accident, so you do not have to call the hospitals. However, if the person did not have their identification with them—such as if they were out for a jog—it is possible that the hospital did not know whom to contact.) If, after you've made these telephone calls, you still have no sign of your loved one, call the police. You have done your homework and, when you call, your case should meet the criteria of a missing person case.

If the police refuse to take a report, ask them to tell you their reasons why. Then, ask to speak to a supervisor. The longer you wait to file a report, your chances of finding your loved one safe and sound may diminish. Every minute counts.

If your missing loved one does not meet the criteria for the AMBER Alert or EMPA, don't despair. At that point, cooperate with the investigating law agency and then begin to conduct your own search.

Look for clues to help find your missing loved one. Look for their belongings. Did they leave their car, keys, cell phone, purse or wallet, bankcards and/or money? Did they leave behind any other personal belongings that they always take with them? Did they leave a pet without making arrangements? If it is not customary for the person to leave without taking care of such things, this could signify that their disappearance is involuntary. On the other hand, if these items and a dear pet are gone, you must consider that your loved one might have left voluntarily. You can further investigate this by checking to see if any clothes are missing along with a suitcase, passport, etc.

While you are going through your loved one's belongings, collect the person's toothbrush and a hairbrush or comb. If the police do not initially want these, hold onto them. If your loved one is missing for thirty days, law enforcement will be *required* to enter DNA information into the NCIC national system and to ask you for permission to obtain your loved one's dental records.

If you share a bank account with your missing loved one, you can probably access your account online and look at recent debit card transactions. If you see any activity on the missing person's card, determine the location of the transaction. Is it a customary place for your loved one to use their debit card? In any case, share this information with the investigating officer. Similarly, if you are the account-holder for the cell phone that your loved one uses, call your cell provider and ask if the person's phone has been used since they went missing. (Again, if you have reason to believe that the person was abducted, *do not call the cell phone*, which will likely alert an abductor to the presence of the phone.) If you cannot gain access to bank transactions or cell phone records, the police can, so be proactive. Ask the law enforcement investigator if they are contacting your cellular service provider and your bank.

Many nonprofit organizations provide free services to help families search for a missing person. Do not hesitate to call the groups listed in this chapter—and don't wait too long. Most of these organizations have twenty-four-hour hotlines and they can provide comprehensive resources to help you jumpstart your search. Remember, time is of the essence.

Is Your Child Considering Running Away?

Some children do not broadcast any obvious warning signs or say anything before they leave but, in other cases, you can spot signs that your child is thinking about running away or even making such plans. If you know these signs, you can be alert and try to prevent it from happening. As the parent of a teenager, you can educate yourself on these warning signs and others. Stay involved in your child's life, but be careful not to impede too much on their privacy. In some instances, the more you push, the harder they rebel. Here are some warning signs to notice:

- Changes in behavior, like sneaking out at night, skipping school, increased tardiness, or rebellious or argumentative behavior;
- Changes in the friends with whom your child hangs out;
- New tastes in music, changes in personal style;
- Alcohol or drug use;
- Uncharacteristic mood changes, such as being tired a lot, falling grades or a sudden disinterest in school, personality changes or suicidal indications;
- Increased use of the Internet or telephone (which might signal a child's unhappiness with their current situation and the desire to leave for what they believe is a better life);
- Searching web sites for maps;
- Withdrawing money from accounts;
- Direct red flags, such as threatening to run away or telling friends or others about the idea.

Get the Word Out

Collect recent photos of your missing person and select one photo that clearly shows the person's face. Select a second photo that shows their full body. Make copies of these photos and then provide them to the police.

As soon as possible, you should prepare informative posters to publicize the fact that someone in the community is missing, and to provide the public with details about your missing person so you encourage your neighbors to pay attention to any clues. You want to people to notice your case so they will generate leads that law enforcement can follow up on. Several of the non-profit organizations listed in this chapter will provide you with comprehensive help free of charge to produce these posters; one of these groups is the NCMEC at 1-800-THE-LOST.

Your poster should include the two photos—a clear one of the person's face and a second one that shows the full body. In addition, you should include:

- The missing person's name and date of birth;
- The missing person's physical description;
- Any known information about what the person was last wearing;
- Information about the last time and place anyone saw the person;
- Anything you know about the circumstances by which they went missing;
- Any information about persons who might have been involved in their disappearance;
- Police contact information.

Ask friends and other volunteers to help you to distribute and post these posters. Start locally, concentrating the posters in the area where your loved one was last seen. Then, as you print more posters, expand your distribution to regional areas.

To quickly spread word that your loved one is missing, use the Internet and, particularly, social media. If you are not already a member of some of the social media sites, don't take the time to enroll in them. Instead, give your poster to friends and other volunteers who are members of the various communities, and ask them to initiate a campaign to publicize your case. Each posting should include one or both of the photographs, the basic information from the poster, and a request that the recipients please repost the message.

Finally, contact the media. Call your local newspaper, television and radio reporters and tell them about your missing loved one. Explain the circumstances under which the person went missing and ask if you can email a photograph. Work with your police investigator to handle the media. You want to keep your story on the public's minds so people remain alert and think to call in with any leads. After your initial story, you'll need to be creative to keep your story in the news. Look for different "headlines" to give the press a new angle to cover so they can continue to focus on your missing loved one.

If the story begins to fade, you might offer a reward for information leading to the location of your loved one. *However, be wary of possible exploitation.* Even at such a traumatic time, scammers might prey upon you by claiming that they have information that's vital to the case, and they'll part with this bogus information if you'll just part with your money. Report any such incidents—and all leads—to law enforcement before you pay out any rewards.

National Resources

The Doe Network
www.doenetwork.org
Assists law enforcement in solving cold cases concerning unexplained disappearances and unidentified victims.

National Crime Information Center (NCIC), FBI, Criminal Justice Information Services (CJIS) Division
Clarksburg, West Virginia
304-625-2000
www.fas.org/irp/agency/doj/fbi/is/ncic.htm
Maintains searchable database for law enforcement agencies.

CLEARINGHOUSE: National Center for Missing Adults (NCMA)
Corporate Headquarters: 479-871-1059
Hotline: 800-690-FIND
Registration: register@missingadults.org
General Inquiries: info@missingadults.org
www.theyaremissed.org/ncma/index.php
National clearinghouse for missing adults helps coordinate agencies and provides state, national and international resource lists and national missing-persons database.

National Center for Missing and Exploited Children (NCMEC)
Hotline: 1-800-THE-LOST (800-843-5678)
www.missingkids.com
Helps find missing children and assists victims of abduction/exploitation as well as their families and caregivers.

NamUs—National Missing and Unidentified Persons System
www.namus.gov/index.htm

questions@findthemissing.org
A clearinghouse for missing persons and unidentified decedent records, NamUs also completes DNA testing and forensic services.

National Runaway Switchboard
1-800-RUNAWAY (1-800-786-2929)
www.1800runaway.org
Help for teenagers who are thinking of running away from home, have a friend who has run and needs help, and runaways who are ready to go home.

Association of Missing & Exploited Children's Organizations (AMECO)
703-838-8379 | Toll Free: 877-263-2620
www.amecoinc.org
info@amecoinc.org
An organization of member organizations that provide search support services from case assistance in making flyers and notifying communities.

Social Security Administration (SSA)
Division of Certification and Coverage
800-772-1213
Program helps people contact a missing person without compromising the missing person's privacy. Searchers write a letter and send it to SSA, which will search a database of individuals' names and addresses. If possible, SSA will forward the letter to the person, who can decide whether they wish to respond.

Next-of-Kin Registry
www.pleasenotifyme.org
Global organization provides a free resource for supplying emergency contact information for next of kin.

One Missing Link (OML)
Springfield, MO 65808
417-886-5836 | Toll-Free: 800-555-7037
www.onemissinglink.org
Affiliated with the NCMEC, OML facilitates networking between agencies and assists families with referrals and poster distribution.

Salvation Army
800-698-7728
Offers assistance to the family of an adult who has been missing for more than six months.

America's Most Wanted
www.amw.com
In addition to the television program, AMW provides missing-persons and missing-children search services and other resources. AMW only features cases that have been reported to police; submit cases in writing.

Project Jason
www.projectjason.org
Phone: 402-932-0095
information@projectjason.org
Nonprofit organization provides case assessment, resources, and support for families of the missing.

Polly Klaas Foundation
Hotline: 800-587-4357
www.pollyklaas.org
service@pollyklaas.org

Nonprofit that helps find missing children, works to prevent children from going missing, and promotes laws to help keep children safe.

Operation Lookout: National Center for Missing Youth
Hotline: 1-800-LOOKOUT (800-566-5688)
www.operationlookout.org
casework2@operationlookout.org
Search assistance and family/victim support services.

Community United Effort (CUE) Center for Missing Persons
910-343-1131 | 910-232-1687
www.ncmissingpersons.org
Search services including making posters, printing, search/recovery resources, bulk mailings, case aid requests of law enforcement, and general casework.

The Laura Recovery Center
281-482-LRCF(5723) | Toll Free: 866-898-5723
www.lrcf.org
Works to promote education and prevention and provides search services.

People-Search Websites
www.skipease.com
www.anywho.com
www.rootsweb.com
www.autotrackxp.com

Find the Hospitals in Your Area
These websites facilitate a search of hospitals in a given region or locality, to generate a list of hospitals with their names, addresses and telephone numbers.

www.doctordirectory.com/doctors/directory
www.hospitallink.com
www.helplinedatabase.com/hospital-us/index.html
www.yellowpages.com

Search the Jails in Your Area
This website facilitates a search of jails in a given region, so that you can produce a list of jails with their addresses and telephone numbers.

www.inmatejailsearch.com

State Clearinghouses

ALABAMA

Alabama Bureau of Investigation / Missing Children
Montgomery, AL
800-228-7688
info@dps.state.al.us
www.dps.alabama.gov/abi
www.community.dps.alabama.gov

ALASKA

Alaska State Troopers, Missing Persons Clearinghouse
Anchorage, AK
907-269-5497 | Toll Free: 800-478-9333 (in-state only)
74431.124@compuserve.com
www.dps.state.ak.us
www.dps.alaska.giv/AST/abi/missingpersons.aspx

ARIZONA

Arizona Department of Public Safety, Criminal Investigations Research Unit
Phoenix, AZ
602-223-2158
74431.127@compuserve.com
www.dps.state.az.us
www.arizona.uscity.net/Missing_Persons

ARKANSAS

Office of Attorney General, Missing Children Services Program
Little Rock, AR
501-682-1020 | Toll Free: 800-448-3014 (in-state only)
74431.126@compuserve.com
www.ag.state.ar.us

www.acic.org/missing/imdex.htm

Morgan Nick Foundation, Inc.
Alma, AR 72921
479-632-6382 | Toll Free: 877-543-HOPE (4673)
morgannick@aol.com
www.lbth.org

CALIFORNIA

California Department of Justice, Missing/Unidentified Persons Unit
Sacramento, CA
916-227-3290 | Toll Free: 800-222-3463 (nationwide)
missing.persons@doj.ca.gov
www.ag.ca.gov/missing

Amber Foundation for Missing Children, Inc.
Pinole, CA
510-222-9050 | Toll Free: 1-800-541-0777
amberjeansmom@yahoo.com
www.missingchild.org

Child Quest International, Inc.
San Jose, CA
408-287-4673 (HOPE) | Toll Free: 1-888-818-4673 (HOPE) sightings
info@childquest.org
www.childquest.org

Children of the Night
Van Nuys, CA
818-908-4474 | Toll Free: 1-800-551-1300
llee@childrenofthenight.org
www.childrenofthenight.org

Interstate Association for Stolen Children, Inc.
Rancho Cordova, CA
916-631-7631
iasckids@pacbell.net
www.geocities.com/CapitalHill/6042

The Carole Sund/Carrington Memorial Reward Foundation
Modesto, CA
Toll Free: 888-813-8389
sundfund@thevision.net
www.carolesundfoundation.com

The Joyful Child Foundation in Memory of Samantha Runnion
Westminster, CA
Toll Free: 1-866-756-9385 (866-7JOYFUL)
inquiry@thejoyfulchild.org
www.thejoyfulchild.org

Trinity Search and Recovery
925-918-3669
www.trinitysearch.org/tsar
help@trinitysearch.org
Offers a variety of search services, including volunteer ground, air and/or water searches as well as coordination with law enforcement and media.

COLORADO

Colorado Bureau of Investigation, Missing Person/Children Unit
Denver, CO
303-239-4251
www.cbi.state.co.us

Missing Children's Task Force
Littleton, CO 80163
720-641-6432
childfinders@qwest.net
www.childfinders.org

CONNECTICUT

Connecticut State Police, Missing Persons
Middletown, CT
860-685-8190 | Toll Free: 800-367-5678 (in-state only)
Emergency Mssg: 1-860-685-8190
dps.feedback@po.state.ct.us
www.state.ct.us/dps/csp.htm
www.conneticut.uscity.net/Missing_Persons

The Paul & Lisa Program, Inc.
Westbrook, CT
860-767-7660
plinc@paulandlisa.org
www.paulandlisa.org

DELAWARE

Delaware State Police, State Bureau of Identification
Dover, DE
302-739-5883
74431.133@compuserve.com
www.state.de.us/dsp/sbi.htm#MISSING
www.delaware.uscity.net/Missing_Persons

DISTRICT OF COLUMBIA

D.C. Metropolitan Police Department, Missing Persons/ Youth Division
Washington, DC
202-576-6768
74431.132@compuserve.com
www.mpdc.dc.gov/main.shtm

FLORIDA

Florida Department of Law Enforcement
Missing Children Information Clearinghouse
Tallahassee, FL
850-410-8585 | Toll Free: 1-888-356-4774 (nationwide)
mcic@fdle.state.fl.us
www.fdle.state.fl.us

www.fdle.state.fl.us/pas/person/displayMissingPersonsSearch
www.florida.uscity.net/Missing_Persons

A Child is Missing, Inc.
Ft. Lauderdale, FL
954-763-1288 | Toll Free: 1-888-875-2246 (1-888-US5-ACIM)
acim@mindspring.com
www.achildismissing.org

Child Watch of North America, Inc.
Orlando, FL
407-290-5100 | Toll Free: 1-800-928-2445; 1-888-CHILDWATCH
info@childwatch.org
www.childwatch.org

Jimmy Ryce Center for Victims of Predatory Abduction, Inc.
Miami Beach, FL
305-864-1344
305-864-4161
misujim@netrox.net
www.jimmyryce.org

Missing Children Center, Inc.
Winter Springs, FL
407-327-4403 | Toll Free: 1-800-330-1907
missingchildren@cfl.rr.com
www.missingchildrencenterinc.org

Voice for the Children, Inc.
West Palm Beach, FL
Toll Free: 800-284-3576

MVoice4@aol.com
www.voice4thechildreninc.org

GEORGIA

Georgia Bureau of Investigation, Intelligence Unit
Decatur, GA
404-244-2554 | Toll Free: 800-282-6564 (nationwide)
www.ganet.org/gbi

HAWAII

Missing Child Center—Department of the Attorney General
State Office Tower
Honolulu, HI
808-586-1449 | Hotline: 808-753-9797
800-468-4644 ext. 6-1449 (Neighbor Isle)
hsc@hgea.org
www.launch.hgea.org/hsc
www.hawaii.uscity.net/Missing_Persons

IDAHO

Idaho State Police Special Programs Unit, Missing Persons Clearinghouse
Meridian, ID
208-884-7154 | Toll Free: 888-777-3922 (nationwide)
idmpc@isp.state.id.us
www.isp.state.id.us/identification/missing/index.html

ILLINOIS

Illinois State Police
Springfield, IL
217-785-4341 | Toll Free: 800-843-5763 (nationwide)
missing@isp.state.il.us
www.isp.state.il.us

www.someoneismissing.com/illinois/missing.htm

INDIANA

Indiana State Police, Indiana Missing Children Clearinghouse
Indianapolis, IN
317-232-8310 | Toll Free: 800-831-8953 (nationwide)
isp@isp.state.in.us
www.isp.state.in.us

IOWA

Missing Person Information Clearinghouse, Iowa Division of Criminal Investigation
Des Moines, IA
515-725-6036 | Toll Free: 800-346-5507 (nationwide)
mason@dps.state.ia.us
www.iowaonline.state.ia.us/mpic

KANSAS

Kansas Bureau of Investigation, Missing Persons Clearinghouse
Topeka, KS
785-296-8200
74431.140@compuserve.com
www.accesskansas.org/kbi/mp.htm

KENTUCKY

Kentucky State Police
Frankfort, KY
502-564-1020 | Toll Free: 800-543-7723 (nationwide) or 800-KIDS SAF
74431.141@compuserve.com
www.kentuckystatepolice.org

Exploited Children's Help Organization, Inc.
Louisville, KY
502-636-3670
echolou@aol.com
www.echolou.org

LOUISIANA

*Louisiana Department of Social Services, Clearinghouse for Missing &
Exploited Children, Office of Community Services*
Baton Rouge, LA
225-342-8631
74431.142@compuserve.com
www.dss.state.la.us

MAINE

Maine State Police, Missing Children Clearinghouse
Houlton, ME
207-532-5404
74431.145@compuserve.com
www.state.me.us/msp/msp.htm

MARYLAND

Maryland Center for Missing Children, Maryland State Police—
Computer Crimes Unit
Pikesville, MD
410-290-1620 | Toll Free: 800-637-5437 (nationwide)
TTY 410-486-0677 (deaf or hard of hearing)
marylandch@ncmec.org
www.ccu.mdsp.org/mcmc.htm

Rachel Foundation for Family Reintegration
The Rachel Foundation
Damascus, MD
202-320-0848
contactus@rachelfoundation.org
www.rachelfoundation.org

Missing and Exploited Children's Association (MECA)
Timonium, MD
Toll-Free: 888-755-6322 (MECA)
taavonjm@erols.com
www.mecaofmd.com

MASSACHUSETTS

Massachusetts State Police, Missing Persons Unit
Framingham, MA
Phone: 508-820-2129 | Toll Free: 800-622-5999 (in-state only)
74431.143@compuserve.com
www.state.ma.us/msp

Rad Kids: Personal Empowerment Safety Education
West Harwich, MA
508-430-2080 | Toll Free: 1-866-430-2080
radKIDS@radKIDS.org
www.radKIDS.org

MICHIGAN

Michigan State Police, Prevention Services Unit
East Lansing, MI
517-333-4006 2521 (information) | 24 Hours Emergency: 517-336-6100
76711.3052@compuserve.com
www.michigan.gov/msp

Missing Children's Network of Michigan
Muskegon, MI
616-727-0591 | Toll Free: 800-985-2849
MCNMI@i2k.com
www.i2k.com/~mcnmi

MINNESOTA

Minnesota State Clearinghouse, Bureau of Criminal Apprehension
St. Paul, MN
651-793-1107
74431.146@compuserve.com
www.dps.state.mn.us/bca.bca.html

The Jacob Wetterling Foundation, Metro Office
St. Paul, MN
St. Joseph, MN
651-714-4673 (Edina office) | 320-363-0470 (St. Joseph office)
Toll Free: 800-325-4673 (HOPE)
info@jwf.org
www.jwf.org

Missing Children—Minnesota
Minneapolis, MN
Toll Free: 1-888-786-9355 (RUN-YELL)
mssngchild@aol.com
www.missingchildrenmn.org

MISSISSIPPI

Mississippi Highway Patrol, Criminal Information Center
Pearl, MS
601-933-2659
74431.150@compuserve.com
www.dps.state.mn.us/dps/dps.nsf

MISSOURI

Missouri State Highway Patrol, Missing Persons Unit, Division of Drug and Crime Control
Jefferson City, MO
573-526-6178 | Toll Free: 1-800-877-3452 (nationwide)
missourich@ncmec.org
www.mshp.state.mo.us

One Missing Link
Springfield, MO
417-886-5836 | Toll Free: 1-800-555-7037
onemissinglinkinc@sbcglobal.net
www.onemissinglink.org

MONTANA

Montana Department of Justice, Missing / Unidentified Persons
Helena, MT
406-444-1526
contactdoj@state.mt.us
www.doj.state.mt.us

Christian Lamb Foundation
Powell, WY (Also serves Montana)
307-754-9261 | 800-651-5262
clamb@wavecom.net
www.clamb.org

NEBRASKA

Nebraska Missing Persons Clearinghouse, Nebraska State Patrol Intelligence and Criminal Analysis Division
Lincoln, NE
402-479-4986 | Toll-Free: 1-877-441-5678
missingpersons@nebraska.gov
www.nsp.state.ne.us/missingpersons

NEVADA

Nevada Office of the Attorney General, Missing Children Clearinghouse
Las Vegas, NV
702-486-3539 | Toll Free: 1-800-992-0900 (in-state only)
NEVADACH@ncmec.org
www.ag.state.nv.us/Divisions/FraudUnits/MissingKids/miss_kids.htm

Nevada Child Seekers
Las Vegas, NV
702-458-7009 | Toll Free: 1-877-566-5437

Reno, NV 89502
775-323-5590 | Toll Free: 1-877-566-5437
www.nevadachildseekers.org

NEW HAMPSHIRE

New Hampshire State Police, Investigative Services Bureau, Major Crime Unit
Concord, NH
603-271-2663 | Toll Free: 1-800-852-3411 (in-state only)

24 Hour Referral: 603-271-3636
missingpersons@safety.state.nh.us
www.nh.gov/safety/nhsp

NEW JERSEY

New Jersey State Police, Unidentified Persons Unit
W. Trenton, NJ
609-882-2000 ext 2894 | Toll Free: 800-709-7090 (nationwide)
TRAK#: 609-538-0513
missingp@gw.njsp.org
www.njsp.org/miss/mpu.html

NEW MEXICO

New Mexico Department of Public Safety, Attn: Law Enforcement Records
Santa Fe, NM
505-827-9193
missingpersons@dps.state.mn.us
www.dps.nm.org

NEW YORK

New York Division of Criminal Justice Services, Missing & Exploited Children
Albany, NY
518-457-6326 | Toll Free: 1-800-346-3543 (nationwide)
missingchildren@dcjs.state.ny.us (General E-Mail)
www.criminaljustice.state.ny.us/missing/index.htm

Child Find of America
New Paltz, NY
845-255-1848 | Toll Free: 1-800-I-AM-LOST or 1-800-A-WAY-OUT
information@childfindofamerica.org
www.childfindofamerica.org

The Center for Hope
Ballston Spa, NY
518-884-8761
jdlmary@hope4themissing.org
www.hope4themissing.org

NORTH CAROLINA

North Carolina Center for Missing Persons
Raleigh, NC
919-733-3914 | Toll Free: 1-800-522-5437 (nationwide)
pstewart@ncale.org
www.ncale.org/missingpersons.html

NORTH DAKOTA

North Dakota Clearinghouse for Missing Children, North Dakota Radio Communication
Bismark, ND
701-328-9921 | Toll Free: 800-472-2121 (in-state only)
rhessing@pioneer.state.nd.us
www.state.nd.us/radio//clearing.html

OHIO

Missing Children Clearinghouse, Attorney General's Office, Crime Victims Services Section
Columbus, OH
614-466-5610 | Toll Free: 800-325-5604 (nationwide)
74431.161@compuserve.com
www.mcc.ag.state.oh.us

OKLAHOMA

Oklahoma State Bureau of Investigation, Criminal Intelligence Office
Oklahoma City, OK
405-879-2645 | Toll Free: 800-522-8017
74431.162@compuserve.com
www.osbi.state.ok.us

OREGON

Oregon State Police, Missing Children Clearinghouse
Salem, OR
Phone: 1-503-378-3720 | Toll Free: 1-800-282-7155 (in-state only)
74431.163@compuserve.com
www.osp.state.or.us

PENNSYLVANIA

Pennsylvania State Police, Bureau of Criminal Investigation
Harrisburg, PA
717-783-0960
74431.164@compuserve.com
www.psp.state.pa.us

RHODE ISLAND

Rhode Island State Police, Missing & Exploited Children Unit
North Scituate, RI
401-444-1125 | Toll Free: 1-401-444-1124 (in-state only)
74431.165@compuserve.com
www.risp.state.ri.us/MISSING%20CHILDREN.htm

SOUTH CAROLINA

*South Carolina Law Enforcement Division, Missing Person Information
Center*
Columbia, SC
803-737-9000 | Toll Free: 800-322-4453 (nationwide)
74431.166@compuserve.com
www.sled.state.sc.us/default/htm

SOUTH DAKOTA

*South Dakota Attorney General's Office, Division of Criminal
Investigation*
Pierre, SD
605-773-3331
74431.167@compuserve.com
http://dci.sd.gov/administration/missingpersons.htm

TENNESSEE

Tennessee Bureau of Investigation, Criminal Intelligence Unit
Nashville, TN
615-744-4000 | Toll Free: 1-800-824-3463
74431.170@compuserve.com
www.tbi.state.tn.us

Commission on Missing and Exploited Children (COMEC)
Memphis, TN
901-405-8441
comec@comec.org
www.comec.org

TEXAS

Texas Department of Public Safety, Special Crimes Services, Missing Persons Clearinghouse
Austin, TX
512-424-5074 | Toll Free: 1-800-346-3243 (in-state only)
74431.171@compuserve.com
www.txdps.state.tx.us/mpch

Heidi Search Center
San Antonio, TX
210-650-0428 | Toll Free: 1-800-547-4435
heidisc@flash.net
http://heidisearchcenter.com

The actual MISSING poster (shown here on a local news station) displayed during the eight days Tanya Rider was trapped in her automobile.

The interior of Tanya's vehicle, where she remained trapped for eight days.

Photo by Joshua Trujillo for *Seattle P-I*, furnished by Hearst Corporation.

Photo by Joshua Trujillo for *Seattle P-I*, furnished by Hearst Corporation.

Photo by Joshua Trujillo for *Seattle P-I*, furnished by Hearst Corporation.

Above (two photos) and upper right: Washington State Police examine
the crash scene off Maple Valley Road.

Photo by Joshua Trujillo for *Seattle P-I*, furnished by Hearst Corporation.

Photo by Joshua Trujillo for *Seattle P-I*, furnished by Hearst Corporation.

Police and crew work to remove Tanya Rider's Honda Element from the crash site.

The hilly crash site where Tanya's car was hidden from view.

A yellow van drives by the spot, between the hillside and the telephone pole, where Tanya's car went off the right-hand side of the road into a hidden ravine.

Arriving home from the hospital for the first time, Tanya stands next to her new SUV.

Tanya Rider uses a cane to walk into her house for the first time since the accident.

The Riders on their wedding day.

Tanya with Tom and their dog Lady in 1997.

Tanya and Tom Rider.

Tanya and Tom Rider in March, 2000.

UTAH

Utah Department of Public Safety, Bureau of Criminal Identification
Salt Lake City, UT
801-965-4686 | 801-965-4446 (after hours)
Toll Free: 888-770-6477 (nationwide)
105374.2257@compuserve.com
http://bci.utah.gov/MPC/MPCHome.html

VERMONT

Vermont State Police
Waterbury, VT
802-241-5352
www.dps.state.vt.us/vtsp/index_main.html

VIRGINIA

Virginia State Police Department, Missing Children's Clearinghouses
Richmond, VA
804-674-2000 | 804-674-2026 (24/7 Emergencies only)
Toll Free: 1-800-822-4453
pfagan@vsp.state.va.us
www.vsp.state.va.us/cjis_missing_children.htm

WASHINGTON

Washington State Patrol, Missing Children Clearinghouse
Olympia, WA
Toll Free: 1-800-543-5678 (nationwide)
74431.173@compuserve.com
www.wsp.wa.gov/crime/mcservic.htm

Families and Friends of Missing Persons and Violent Crime Victims
800-346-7555
ContactUs@fnfvcv.org

Operation Lookout: National Center for Missing Youth
Everett, WA
425-771-7335
Toll Free: 800-5688 (LOOKOUT)
Toll Free: 800-782-7335 (SEEK)
casework4@operationlookout.org
www.operationlookout.org

WEST VIRGINIA

West Virginia State Police, Missing Children Clearinghouse
South Charleston, WV
304-558-1467 | Toll Free: 800-352-0927 (nationwide)
MISSINGCHILDREN@wvsp.state.wv.us
www.wvstatepolice.com/children/children.shtml

WISCONSIN

Wisconsin Department of Justice, Division of Criminal Investigation
Madison, WI
608-266-1671 | Toll Free: 1-800-THE-HOPE (in-state only)
wimissingchild@doj.state.wi.us
www.doj.state.wi.us

Youth Educated in Safety, Inc.
PO Box 3124
Appleton, WI 54914

920-734-5335 | Toll Free: 1-800-272-7715
jay@yeswi.org
www.yeswi.org

A Missing Child is Everyone's Responsibility, Operation L.A.P. Foundation, Inc.
Fort Atkinson, WI
Milwaukee: 414-208-8954
Fort Atkinson/Jefferson: 920-674-6960

Wisconsin Center for Missing Children & Adults (WCMCA)
Jefferson, WI
Toll Free: 877-70-5456
24 Hour Crisis: 920-220-1558
wcmca@idcnet.com
www.wcmckids.org

WYOMING

Wyoming Office of the Attorney General, Division of Criminal Investigation
Cheyenne, WY
307-777-7537 | Control Terminal: 307-777-7545
74431.174@compuserve.com
www.attorneygeneral.state.wy.us/dci/index.html

Christian Lamb Foundation
Powell, WY
307-754-9261 | 800-651-5262
clamb@wavecom.net
www.clamb.org

As Time Goes By

You might want to create a web page for your missing person, linking this to other missing person's pages and, perhaps, organizations for missing persons. Many of the organizations listed in this chapter are good resources for such pages and you can update this information with current Internet searches.

If the local police are out of leads and your loved one remains missing, you will need to manage more of the search yourself. But, after your loved one has been missing for thirty days, the police are *legally obligated* to enter your loved one's DNA and dental information into the NCIC database, so you will need to provide this information. You might also need check with the police to make sure that they are following through. Similarly, every year, the police are required to update the file so you might want to renew contact with the police department to make sure that they are doing so.

These systems initiate investigations with coroners and medical examiners to make comparisons with unidentified persons—those who have died and whose bodies have not been identified. For example, the National Missing and Unidentified Persons System automatically performs cross-matching comparisons between databases, searching for matches or similarities between unidentified persons and those who have been reported as missing. Anyone can search this database, which uses characteristics such as sex, race and distinct body features as well as dental records, DNA testing, anthropology, and odontology assistance.

Many organizations can help you continue to follow up. We suggest you contact the organizations listed in this chapter to help you further your search. Private investigators are another option and many are starting to specialize in missing person tracking. Regardless of the age of your missing person, do not hesitate to contact NCMEC for referrals and strategy.

Coping

Sometimes, months, years or even decades go by without word from a missing loved one. This is a brutal time to endure. You will run the gamut of emotions, from sadness and hurt to anger and depression—and everything in between. You may lose your appetite and lose weight. You may have trouble sleeping, be unable to concentrate and even be plagued by violent thoughts of hurting yourself or others. Not uncommonly, family members and close friends of missing persons fall into deep depressions, lose their jobs, neglect other loved ones, and undergo unusual behavior changes. So, although it will be very difficult, you will need to take care of yourself so you can stay strong. To this end, you will need to get help in dealing with your emotions.

A variety of doctors, therapists and other resources can help you cope with the loss of a missing loved one. Family, friends and clergy, in addition to medical professionals, have great listening ears and it is a good step in the right direction to talk to others about your emotions and about your missing loved one. What's more, such consultants can point you to additional help, organizations or professionals whom you might need.

Support groups are also an important resource as they help you connect with organizations full of people in your position. Some members of support groups have positive stories of how their loved one returned home, while others are still on the hunt for theirs. Either way, members of support groups have been where you are. They know what you are experiencing. They can also give you ideas and leads to help you get the word out about your missing loved one and, together, you can help each other to do everything possible to bring your loved one home.

In addition to mental health professionals and emotional support, medical doctors should be included in your self-care effort. Especially if you have a loss of appetite and sleep, it is important that you check in with your doctor. Stress and anxiety about the safe return of your loved one can bring you down and result in further ailments.

No matter what your circumstances, remember: You are not alone. The following organizations can help to connect you with other people in your area who are struggling with similar issues. They can also direct you to local resources and help you find professionals who can help you.

National Support Resources

Association of Missing and Exploited Children's Organization (AMECO)
703-838-8379 | Toll Free: 877-263-2620
www.amecoinc.org
info@amecoinc.org
An organization of member organizations that provides prevention programs and educational materials.

Community United Effort (CUE) Center For Missing Persons
910-343-1131 / 910-232-1687
www.ncmissingpersons.org
Support services include individual/group grief counseling and assistance to meet family's personal needs.

Let's Bring Them Home
National Center for Missing Adults Support Group
Bentonville, AR
Corporate Headquarters: 479-871-1059
www.theyaremissed.org/ncma

National Center for Missing and Exploited Children (NCMEC)
www.missingkids.com
Assists victims of abduction/exploitation and helps their families and caregivers.

One Missing Link (OML)
Springfield, MO
800-555-7037 or 417-886-5836
www.onemissinglink.org
Facilitates networking between agencies and assists families with counseling, emotional support.

Operation Lookout: National Center for Missing Youth
Hotline: 1-800-LOOKOUT (800-566-5688)
www.operationlookout.org
casework2@operationlookout.org
Search assistance and family/victim support services.

Project Jason
Phone: 402-932-0095
www.projectjason.org
information@projectjason.org
Case assessment, resources, and support for families of the missing.

Trinity Search and Recovery
925-918-3669
www.trinitysearch.org
help@trinitysearch.org

Remembering Someone Who is Missing

The website for the organization Let's Bring Them Home/ The National Center for Missing Adults provides helpful ideas for ways families can deal with the trauma of having a loved one disappear. The organization suggests that people can work on continuing to feel close to their missing loved one. To this end, the website provides a list of fifty suggestions for ways you can continue your relationship with your missing loved one.[2]

1. Say your loved one's name out loud and don't be afraid to talk about him or her
2. Keep photos around
3. Write a letter
4. Turn your porch light on at night, until your missing loved one returns
5. Plan an event such as a candlelight vigil, memorial, or balloon release
6. Occasionally eat their favorite food
7. Imagine having a conversation with your missing loved one
8. Say prayers
9. Visit their favorite spot
10. Donate to your loved one's favorite charity
11. Volunteer at your loved one's favorite charity
12. Sometimes when a new building is being erected, you can personalize a brick with your loved one's name
13. Share favorite memories with other family members, especially young children who may not remember the missing person well

14. Create a memory box with a photo, favorite cologne/perfume, piece of clothing, favorite book, and other things that remind you of your loved one

15. Occasionally look through the memory box you've created for your missing loved one

16. Plant flowers or a garden

17. Make a tile or tile wall with your loved one's name and put it in your garden

18. At holidays, birthdays, or other special occasions, give a memento to other family members such as a hat, a shirt, watch, earrings, or a framed photo

19. Keep a diary or journal

20. Paint a picture of your loved one

21. Call other family members or friends of the loved one on their birthday, holidays, or annual date of disappearance

22. Send flowers to another family member on special days

23. Create a new tradition or ritual such as lighting candles every day, week, or month

24. Fly a kite with a special message to your loved one attached

25. Listen to your loved one's favorite song or album

26. Plant a tree and put ribbons on it with family and friends' names and special messages

27. Play your missing loved one's favorite board or video game

28. Create a scrapbook with photos, ticket stubs, poems, letters, and other special items

29. Dedicate a park bench to your missing loved one

30. Make a special ornament or decoration for the holidays with your loved one's name

31. Draw a picture of your loved one

32. Have a celebration for your loved one and invite friends and family to talk about their favorite moments with the missing person

33. Name a star after your missing loved one; they may be looking up at it too
34. Sing a song
35. Write a poem
36. Send balloons to another family member on special days
37. Wear a missing loved one's shirt, hat, or other piece of clothing
38. At holidays and other special occasions, leave an empty chair for the person
39. Make a quilt using scraps of your missing loved one's blankets or clothing
40. Display a special box on your missing loved one's birthday, annual date of disappearance, and holidays and have family and friends fill it with notes.
41. Play your missing loved one's favorite sport
42. Wear a pin with a photo of your missing loved one
43. Read your missing loved one's favorite book or story
44. Continue your missing loved one's favorite tradition
45. Have a calendar made with photos of your missing loved one
46. Follow a rainbow to see if your missing loved one is on the other side
47. Wear clothing with your loved one's favorite color
48. Donate your loved one's favorite book to a library
49. Create a website dedicated to your missing loved one
50. Release a balloon with a special message to your missing loved one

CHAPTER FOUR

What If YOU Are the One Who Is Missing?

It can happen to anybody. You're on the way home from work when your car goes off the road, hidden from other vehicles. You might be alone, trapped, even seriously injured. You will almost certainly be scared. And, worse, you could be stranded for hours or days before someone finds you. What do you do?

And what if you are abducted—grabbed by someone who throws you into the trunk of their car, or chains you to their steering column? What can you do? The best way to survive such an emergency is to be prepared for whatever might happen to you.

Be Prepared

In a car, your survival odds are best when you've prepared for possible emergencies so you have a plan of action and basic tools to support your survival and rescue. With the introduction of technological innovations, motorists have a decisive advantage. Vehicle assistance programs like OnStar can alert authorities that a person needs help, and GPS units can guide you out of dangerous situations, help you figure out where you are if you are lost, and may be able to set off an alarm. But you never know when a high-tech gadget will malfunction or lose power, so low-tech and no-tech tools are also extremely important and valuable. A good, old-fashioned map, for example, could save your life.

Motorists should equip their cars with emergency kits, carried in the trunk at all times. Your emergency kit should include:

- A map of the area in which you are driving;
- A charged cell phone and mobile charger;
- Emergency supplies;
- Drinking water to last for several days;
- High-calorie snacks like candy bars, nuts, energy bars, etc.
- Spare blankets and extra clothing in cold weather; hat and long-sleeved lightweight clothing in hot weather;
- A standard first-aid kit;
- A flashlight with extra batteries;
- A candle, matches and flares.

Of course, your cell phone might be the most important survival tool you own. Every time you get in your vehicle, be sure your phone is well charged. Keep a mobile charger in your car in case your phone's battery runs low.

While driving, be aware of your surroundings. Take note of public places and emergency call boxes along the roadside because, even if you have a cell phone, you might need to find a call box. If you drive out of range of cell service, your phone loses power, or your phone is lost or damaged in a crash, you will be grateful if you know which direction to walk for a call box or other aid.

If you get lost in a rough neighborhood, you are always safer if you remain inside your vehicle. Keep your cell phone handy and lock your doors. Try to retrace your path but also try to stay in populated, well lit areas where people—witnesses—can see you.

If your vehicle is disabled, remain inside, keep your car locked with the windows up, and use your cell phone to call for help. If you are in danger in an urban area or someone is threatening you, lay on the horn to attract attention and call 911; "smart phones" are equipped to transmit digital information about your location so that a dispatcher can determine your location and send the police to help you. If for some reason your cell phone does not work, pretend it does. Look at the person who is threatening you and talk into your cell phone—whether it is connected to another person or not—while you pretend to describe the assailant to the police. Predators have no way to know if you really are on the phone or not, so this may deter them from victimizing you.

Surviving in Your Car

If you have an accident or become stranded in your vehicle on a highway, in a rural area, or in any other safe neighborhood, immediately turn on your hazard lights to alert other vehicles. If you are not in a remote area, a passing car or pedestrian will likely spot your flashing lights and come to your assistance within minutes or hours.

If you have a cell phone and are able to use it, call for help. If you are without a working phone and you are able to walk, set out to find an emergency call box along the road if these are available, or toward any public business. Leave your phone on but turn off the vibration mode, which uses more battery.

The weather—cold or hot—plays a major part in what to do if you are stranded. If you are stuck in your vehicle or outside during cold weather, you must be mindful of a number of physical ailments that can set in. Even when the temperature is above freezing, hypothermia is a risk. It can be fatal. If you do not treat hypothermia soon, your body may undergo cardiac arrest or you could go into shock. Therefore, before you drive in winter conditions, it is important that you prepare by stocking your emergency kit with additional materials specifically to help prevent hypothermia. Extra blankets and warm clothing are mandatory. Also, a candle and matches are compact and extremely helpful items for a wintertime emergency kit, as you can light the candle and warm the interior of your car.

On the other hand, if you are stranded in hot weather, your primary concern will be water and keeping yourself hydrated. Tanya Rider's eight-day survival while trapped in her car is considered a miracle. Most people cannot survive more than about three days without water, though this depends on many factors. In any case, it is easy, especially in hot weather, to become dehydrated.

Keep in mind that, in addition to losing water via elimination (urinating) and perspiration (sweating), our bodies lose water through respiration—breathing. If you understand how you can minimize your body's water loss, you can increase your odds of surviving in the event that you are stranded without a water supply. To reduce your water loss:

- Try not to work up a sweat, even though you must try to get to safety;
- Try not to work so strenuously that you breathe heavily, because this increases your water loss through respiration;
- Try not to panic and breathe heavily and rapidly, as you will lose more water via increased respirations;
- Try to stay as cool as possible to minimize sweating;
- Try to keep your skin out of the sun, as sunburn makes the body lose water more rapidly;
- Avoid exposure to (hot or cold) wind, which wicks moisture away from the body;
- Eat only what you need to keep up your strength. You are better off not eating much, since the body consumes water to digest food;
- Do not consume coffee, alcohol or other diuretics—if you happen to have them with you—because they cause the body to lose water.

What if y You're Stranded Without a Car?

First, stay calm. Stressing about your situation isn't going to make things any better. You'll need a clear and level mind to take in your surroundings and to consider your predicament logically and strategically. What do you see? What do you hear? What do you smell? Are you hurt? Is someone else hurt? Do you have anything that might help you—food, clothing, water, a cell phone?

After you consider your surroundings, make a plan. Contemplate whether you are better off staying put and awaiting help or physically moving out of the area. Either way, decide soon and act quickly. If you sustained any significant injuries, it is probably best to stay stationary and conserve your energy. However, if possible, move to the most visible location in your immediate area. If you believe that people are quite likely to be searching for you in the area, remain as visible as you can and stay in one place so that you are not a moving target. Unless you need to wear all of your clothes for warmth, put any bright garments or other possessions, such as a purse or backpack, out in a clearing or on a tree branch where they will be more visible to anyone who might be searching for you.

If you are caught outdoors for an extended period of time, you'll need to consider a number of factors, such as lack of shelter, poisonous plants, limited food and water supply and the possible presence of dangerous wildlife. To survive, you'll generally need to meet your body's four basic needs: warmth, food, water and sleep.

Warmth. Even if you are in an area with warm daytime weather, when night falls, so does the temperature. While it is light out, try to find a shelter—an abandoned building, cave, or even dense shrubbery that you can crawl under to find some protection from the elements, especially rain. If nothing like this is available, and since weather can be unpredictable, you may need to build some sort of shelter to shield you from the elements, especially if you are caught in a rain shower or snowstorm. If it looks like you will be out overnight, try to build a shelter using foliage from the terrain.

If you do not have enough warm clothing or blankets with you, or you cannot find a shelter, you can keep yourself warm if you know any of several ways to start a fire in the wilderness. It is a good idea to study and practice fire-building techniques before you find yourself in a life-or-death situation. Try to carry matches with you whenever you hike, travel through the country, or in any situation that could possibly leave you stranded out in the elements. It is a good idea to tightly wrap a book of matches in a plastic bag, squeezing out all the air you possibly can before you securely seal the bag with a rubber band. Then, wrap and secure the matches a second time, so that the packet is waterproof. If you are going to be away from civilization, carry this packet in your wallet, purse, backpack or pocket. Something as small and simple as a book of matches could save your life.

Water. Water is essential for life and you can only survive without it for a matter of days. But drinking dirty water can cause a number of ailments (including diarrhea, which causes more loss of hydration) so you should think about different ways to locate water and to purify it for drinking and cooking. If it rains, use a large leaf to devise a bowl so you can catch rainwater, or lay a shirt out to soak up rain and then suck the water out of the shirt. Usually, at dusk, deer and other wild animals descend to their water supplies. If you study animal-made tracks in the earth, you might be able to see animal tracks that could lead you to a natural source of water.

Food. You can survive without food for up to three weeks. However, if you are in the wilderness for an extended period of time, you will need the energy that food provides in order to work on your survival and rescue. Therefore, the most valuable thing you can do, in advance of any such emergency, is to become acquainted with the native food sources in the region in which you are traveling. Tossing a guidebook about poisonous and edible plants into your purse or backpack could save your life. Nuts and berries can provide precious calories on which you can sustain yourself. You might try to devise a weapon or build a trap so that you can hunt or trap an animal for food. If productive, this food can sustain you for an extended period of time.

Sleep. Of course, you will want to get back to your nice warm house and see your loved ones as soon as possible, but that does not mean you should travel all day and all night. Your body needs rest. Without it, you could suffer from exhaustion, which will only hinder your ability to get back to safety. Listen to your body and rest when you need to. If you do not have any sort of shelter in which to sleep, try to lean your back up against a large rock, hill, or other natural protuberance, if possible. This way, if an animal comes near you, it cannot approach you from behind.

Abduction

When a person is abducted—whether the victim is a child or an adult—they can do several things to increase their chances of rescue and survival. It is a good idea to review these tips periodically so that, if you are caught in such a situation, you can recall these suggestions and react quickly.

Of course, it would be best if you can avoid being captured in the first place. The following suggestions should always be on your mind so that, if you find yourself threatened, they are automatic reactions to the situation:

- If you are driving and someone is following you, drive to the nearest police department or hospital.
- If someone is approaching you, use your car horn to draw attention to yourself and to your potential abductor.
- Your greatest weapon is your voice. Make as much noise as possible.

However, do not yell anything about a weapon—even if the abductor is using one—and do not yell "Help me!" Instead, yell "Fire!" or "I am being abducted!"

- If you have any bulky objects with you, hold on tight and use these items to obstruct an abductor who is trying to shove you into a car. For example, if you have a bicycle, grip a bar on the bike and do not let go, the abductor cannot force you *and* your bicycle into the vehicle. If you have a purse or backpack that has straps, hold onto the bag and try to hook the straps onto the door or other obstacles in order to obstruct the abductor from wrestling you into the car.

If a predator succeeds in abducting you, you must do all you can to escape before you are taken to a private place. While you are being transported, look for opportunities to alert passersby that you are in trouble:

- Call attention to yourself and your potential abductor, even if you need to break the law. (These are FBI guidelines!) Drive the wrong way on a one-way road, run a red light, lightly tap your foot on the brake pedal so the brake lights blink on and off, subtly weave the car so you look like a drunk driver. Do anything you can to attract attention. If nothing works, in a final act of desperation, purposely crash your car in an occupied area. Your odds of surviving a low-speed crash are better than surviving an abduction.
- If you are imprisoned in the trunk of a car, unplug the wiring to the rear lights or punch out the plastic cover on the car's lights and stick your arm out of the trunk.
- Create a trail by dropping as much evidence as you possibly can. Drop pieces of clothing or personal belongings. If you can pull out and drop pieces of your hair, search dogs might be able to pick up on these; this has been successful for some in the past. Even spit or blood can be helpful. If you are menstruating, leave pieces of soiled Kotex or

a used tampon to be found. Any personal items, jewelry or DNA is potentially helpful.

- Grab anything you can off the attacker, including jewelry.
- If you break free from your abductor, run in a zig-zag pattern. Turn a corner if you can. If you are in a city area with buildings, try to turn a corner and, as quickly as possible, look for a door into a building.

Deciding whether to fight or not is a personal decision; no one should ever be criticized for deciding not to fight. However, if you decide to fight, you must fight with the intention of escaping, harming and/or killing your abductor. Anything less than a fully committed intention and effort will backfire, increasing the odds that you will be injured or killed. If you choose to fight, you will only survive if you fight to win. Whether your attacker or abductor is male or female, target the eyes, head and groin, which are the most vulnerable areas.

Important Cell Phone Smarts

Cell phones can be a very powerful and effective tool in rescuing a person who has been abducted. Unfortunately, predators know this. Still, you can do a couple of things to maintain possession of your cell phone for as long as possible:

- Leave your cell phone turned on. As long as the phone is on, we have a chance to capture the cell tower or even the precise location of the phone itself. When you or your abductor turn off the phone, we have no chance to trace it.
- PUT YOUR PHONE IN SILENT MODE. As soon as abductors become aware that a captive has a cell phone, they will turn it off or dispose of it—or both.
- Since it is a distinct possibility than an abductor will strip you, do not hide your cell phone in your clothes or shoes. The best place to hide

139

your phone is within your hair, if this is at all possible, because even if you are stripped, it is unlikely that the abductor will search your head. If you can tuck the phone into the hair under a ponytail or tie your phone to the hair next to your neck, your phone is least likely to be found.

- Many abductors demand that their captors turn over their phone. If you have an old cell phone that you're not using, consider bringing it as a decoy whenever you travel alone. This way, if an abductor takes you and demands that you surrender your cell phone, you can surrender your non-operating decoy phone. This should at least buy you a little more time with your phone and, perhaps, allow you to keep your working phone with you and turned on.

When Escape Is Not an Option

The first forty-five minutes of an abduction are the most dangerous and the most volatile. During this time, you can increase your chances of survival if you make your abductor see you as a human and not as an object. To this end, you can manipulate the situation by expressing yourself to your captor:

- Being quiet makes you an easy target and a victim. Even if your abductor tells you to be quiet, do not be quiet. Talk! Make noise and communicate with your abductor. This makes you more of a challenge and the abductor will possibly release you to choose an easier target.
- The more you can get your abductor to relate to you or to value you as a person, the better your chance at survival. Try to interact with the abductor and to establish a person-to-person relationship. Just as, in the development of the Stockholm Syndrome, captives can develop positive feelings for their captors, the reciprocal of this can also happen: Captors can develop positive feelings for their captives. If you can create this situation, it can save your life.

The Stockholm Syndrome is a psychological phenomenon in which hostages develop positive feelings for their abductors and, simultaneously, they develop negative feelings toward the police and other authorities who prosecute their abductors. An important third aspect of the Stockholm Syndrome is that abductors also develop positive feelings toward their hostages! This is where the Stockholm Syndrome can be useful in saving your life if you become a victim of an abduction. At times, the Stockholm Syndrome develops very quickly and, as hostage negotiators, we are encouraged to create it in a short period of time.

In hostage negotiations, I want to create a human factor so I would try to foster a relationship between the captor and myself, as well as between the abductor and the victim. For example, we hostage negotiators press the hostage-taker or abductor to assess a captive, forcing him or her to view the victim as an individual. We also provide "family style" food and drinks, such as a pizza or sandwich fixings and two-liter-size bottles of soda with cups, instead of cans. This manipulates the hostage-taker, forcing them to interact with hostages and encouraging development of the psychological connection between them. That connection can save captives' lives.

Therefore, if you are abducted, you should take these same sorts of measures to try to create a connection between your captor and yourself. Get the person to see you as an individual. Talk about yourself, what you do and what your life is like. Get the person to see you as an individual. Tell the person your name. Share family names, photos, stories, dreams, and goals. Tell them that you are hungry and talk about what you like to eat. Say anything about yourself as a person. And ask the abductor what his or her name is and, if you get this information, use the person's name and see if you can get any other personal information from them.

As soon as you can, in the beginning stages, you need to determine the answers to three questions:

- Who has you?
- What do they want?
- What are they willing to do?

Determining who has you and what they want will help you determine a plan for escape and also gives you an idea of how much time you might have. If you are dealing with a sexual predator, what they want will, unfortunately, be obvious. But this also means you may have some time on your side. If a serial killer has you, you have little time; you will have to act more recklessly to make your escape. If someone takes you in the hopes of stealing money from your bank accounts and then disposing of you, your best hope is to delay the process and create more time for escape by giving them the wrong access codes.

In order to survive the process of being missing, *action* is the most important thing. More than anything else, action can impact whether you will live through the ordeal. To do nothing ensures failure, both for the missing person and for those who are searching and trying to rescue them.

Time is always critical and every hour counts. Therefore, if a loved one is missing, DO NOT wait to call the police and file a report. *There is no twenty-four-hour rule!* And, if it is you who becomes missing, *immediately* start planning your escape—and work on implementing that plan right away so you can return to your loved ones!

CHAPTER FIVE

Dr. Carole's Couch: Overcoming Trauma

By Carole Lieberman, M.D.

Ah, the stories I have heard from people sitting on my couch. How often I have wished that others could be flies on the wall and hear the tales of tragedy and triumph, suffering and survival that spill out amidst the tears and anxious laughter.

How do we find the wherewithal to go on living after we have experienced traumatic events or been brushed by people who cause us pain? Even before we are born, the emotions felt by our mother during pregnancy find their way into the womb. And once we are born, it seems like life is a minefield, with countless traumas just waiting for us to step on them. Abandonment. Accident. Bankruptcy. Breakup. Cheating spouse. Child abuse. Death of a loved one. Divorce. Failure. Illness or injury. Impotence. Incest. Infertility. Job loss. Mental illness. Man-made disaster. Natural disaster. Rape. Robbery. Terrorism. Violence. Widowhood… and so much more—a veritable alphabet of catastrophes. When they blow up our world, how do we put the pieces back together?

Our mind works like a video camera, capturing all the sights and sounds and feelings of our life—and storing them in a permanent private collection. Our mind also protects us from the stored memories that are the most painful. These repressed memories are buried in our unconscious, so that they don't intrude into each subsequent moment of our everyday lives. Otherwise, we would be flooded by them. But, these memories can still burst into consciousness when something triggers them: the smell of aftershave that our father wore, a photograph found at the bottom of a drawer, a visit to our hometown, old love letters from a spouse who went on to cheat, a finger-painting from a deceased child, the taste of cookies a mother used to make before she abandoned her family, the still-gaping wound in lower Manhattan where the Twin Towers once stood.

Keeping our painful memories buried takes an insidious psychological and physical toll on us. The psychological energy needed to keep them under wraps is then not available for other psychological tasks, such as being able to experience a full range of emotions and being fully present for those we care about. Over time, the stress of keeping memories buried also affects our physical health, contributing to problems from hives to high blood pressure and from cancer to cardiac arrest.

What makes it worse is when we hide behind the psychological defense mechanism of denial. We tell ourselves that we are "happy" or "lucky" that we don't remember because the event or the person who hurt us isn't worth it or is better forgotten, as if we can make the trauma disappear by willing it to be so. Then the work of putting the calamity in perspective, growing, surviving and thriving is made so much more complicated, like playing peek-a-boo with the pain.

When something bad befalls us, the natural reaction is to ask, "Why?" and "How did it happen?" We want to understand so that it doesn't happen again. And we want to blame others for our misfortune. Sometimes, it is obvious who is responsible. Often, we also blame our loved ones for not protecting us from harm. Many of us blame God or the universe, and scream silently towards the heavens, "Why me God? What did I do to deserve this?" The sad little secret is that, regardless of whomever else we blame, we blame ourselves the most and feel guilty for our real or imagined trespasses that we suspect brought on the pain.

It often feels like bad things happen when things have been going well, too well. When we're feeling like life has finally turned around, things are looking up and we're certain it will be rosy from now on. It's times like these when a mine explodes and shatters our world to pieces. This teaches us to become fearful, whenever good things come into our lives, that there will be a high price to pay. When we were little and put our hand in the cookie jar or made a loud ruckus having fun with our friends, we were punished. So, now, we can't help wondering if we are guilty of some harmless mischief that will merit a more dreadful punishment. After enough of these roller-coaster rides—the ups and downs of life—it's tempting to give up. We're taunted by the feeling that bad things are bound to follow on the heels of good ones, and that we are destined to lose.

As a general rule, the more nurtured and loved, and less traumatized, our childhood has been, the more psychologically hardy and resilient we grow up to be. But there are exceptions. Some people have a will to survive that surmounts even the most horrendous childhoods.

Friedrich Nietzsche, a nineteenth century philosopher, wrote, "That which does not kill us makes us stronger."[1] His life was filled with traumatic events: the death of his father when he was four years old, the death of his brother when Friedrich was five, career disappointments, the lack of success for his literary works, unrequited love, illnesses and injuries that caused pain and debility. And, yet, he held on to not only the will to live but also the crusade to achieve greatness. Each tragedy made him more tenacious and determined. He defined life itself as having an instinct for growth and strength. And though, ultimately, he was overtaken by madness and death, he left a legacy of writings and posthumous influence that would have made him proud.

Today, over a hundred years later, we repeat Nietzsche's words, "That which does not kill us makes us stronger," under our breath like a mantra, when we are struggling through tough times. We want to believe there is a reason, a purpose for our suffering. And we try to comfort others with this, as well. But there are caveats to this aphorism. We should not deny our vulnerability, nor our past pain, even as we are making efforts to heal.

The most classic quotes about surviving adversity come from people whose lives have forced them to ponder this conundrum for themselves.

Former First Lady Eleanor Roosevelt spoke from personal life lessons when she said, "You gain strength, courage and confidence by every experience in which you really stop to look fear in the face."[2] By age ten, Eleanor had become an orphan. She was starved for attention and considered herself ugly. She learned of her husband's first affair when she discovered love letters in his suitcase.

Franklin went on to have other lovers, despite having become paralyzed. Retaining her dignity throughout, Eleanor asserted, "Women are like teabags. We don't know our true strength until we are in hot water."

"Even as the stone of the fruit must break, that its heart may stand in the sun, so must you know pain.... Accept the seasons of your heart, even as you have always accepted the seasons that pass over your fields."[3] Khalil Gibran, best known for his poetic treatise *The Prophet*, has known pain from the time he was a young boy in Lebanon, and his father's gambling debts and imprisonment forced his family to become homeless. His mother took him and his siblings to America. When he was approximately nineteen years old, his sister, half-brother and mother died, leaving him almost completely alone in this still unfamiliar country.

Media mogul Oprah Winfrey advises us to, "Turn your wounds into wisdom."[4] And, indeed, she has done just that. Her childhood was replete with wounds, including being born to unmarried teen parents who soon split and abandoned her, living in abject poverty, being repeatedly sexually abused, becoming pregnant as a teen and experiencing her son's death shortly after birth. Yet she has managed to surmount all of this pain to achieve immeasurable success and offer wisdom to others.

"We shall draw from the heart of suffering itself the means of inspiration and survival,"[5] former Prime Minister Sir Winston Churchill reassured us. Born two months prematurely, in the nineteenth century, Churchill had to fight for his own survival from the beginning. Though he begged his mother to visit him at school or to allow him to come home, she and his father kept their distance from him. Churchill also suffered from a speech impediment. From his own experience he recommended, "If you are going through hell, keep going."[6]

"I have heard there are troubles of more than one kind. Some come from ahead and some come from behind, But I've bought a big bat. I'm all ready you see. Now my troubles are going to have troubles with me!"[7] Who else but Dr. Seuss, also known as Theodor Seuss Geisel, could put it so humorously and make us laugh at ourselves? Yet, even this award-winning children's book author had obstacles he had to surmount. He was born into a wealthy family who suffered a sudden change of circumstances when his father inherited the family brewery one month before the start of Prohibition. In college, he was caught hosting a party in his room where alcohol was served and the dean insisted he resign from all extra-curricular activities, including his editorship of the college humor magazine. His first wife committed suicide. And his first children's book was rejected almost thirty times. It took years for him to attain success. Yet today, children worldwide still giggle over *The Cat in the Hat* and *Horton Hatches the Egg*.

"When it is dark enough, you can see the stars,"[8] Ralph Waldo Emerson, a nineteenth-century lecturer and writer, tells us. There were many dark days for him. Not only did three of his siblings die in childhood, his father died before Emerson was eight years old. Later, two younger brothers and his first wife died from tuberculosis. But he continued searching for the stars, and went on to have a fine career as an intellectual voice.

"We must try not to sink beneath our anguish... but battle on,"[9] according to J.K. Rowling, the British author whose *Harry Potter* series has taken the world by storm. She had been working as a secretary when the idea for a story about a young boy attending a school of wizardry came to her. Before she could finish writing the first book, her mother died after a long battle with multiple sclerosis. Next, her marriage crumbled just months after her daughter was born. Jo contemplated suicide and was diagnosed with depression. Fortunately, she did "battle on" and her extraordinary rags-to-riches story began. From bleak days, dependent upon welfare and writing *Harry Potter* on an old manual typewriter, she has become a billionaire, lauded for encouraging children to return to the art of reading.

So what are we to do when the ill winds of fortune blow in our direction? The answer isn't to stay cuddled up under the covers, hoping to hide from the gusts as they pass overhead. That's not living. But there are things we can do to survive and even triumph over tragedy.

The most basic thing to remember is to breathe, slowly and deeply. When we become frightened, we start taking short shallow breaths. We may even hold our breath. Our brain and the rest of our body need oxygen to function. When we concentrate on our breathing and focus on taking slow, deep breaths, we naturally relax.

"Through humor, you can soften some of the worst blows that life delivers. And once you find laughter, no matter how painful your situation might be, you can survive it,"[10] according to comedian Bill Cosby. When we can laugh at our own foibles or the irony of the universe, our pent-up tension is defused and we begin to find creative solutions.

Losing ourselves in a passion—such as running, riding horses, art, music, poetry, or film—is a soothing escape that gives us perspective when we get back to the task of solving our problems.

Living with a pet helps change the focus from us wanting to be taken care of to our taking care of another living creature. Our pets love us unconditionally, sensing when we are sad and becoming more loving to comfort us.

Self-help books are invaluable because we can live vicariously through the stories of other people's struggles to survive, and find solace. Similarly, self-help groups can be useful because it is comforting to find a supportive ear when recounting experiences that were embarrassing or devastating.

Keeping a gratitude journal reminds us that we have much to be thankful for, despite the dark clouds hovering over us at the moment.

Meditating and keeping a diary help to bring traumatic memories to the forefront. Similarly, guided imagery is a psychotherapeutic tool that brings memories back in the form of waking dreams, whose symbolism can be interpreted much like the symbols of dreams that we have when we are asleep.

It takes time to process our traumatic experiences in a slow, careful manner, so as to call up the repressed memories and feel the feelings, a little at a time. This is what is done in psychotherapy. Although re-experiencing the pain is not pleasant at first, it soon becomes extremely cathartic and liberating.

The key is to grow through all of these therapeutic endeavors until the memories have lost their painful charge. We must not allow ourselves to be defined by one or more traumatic events from our past. Instead, we must surround ourselves with warm-hearted people, who are as devoted to loving us as we are to loving them. And we must dedicate ourselves with renewed vigor to making happier and more fulfilling new memories each day, which will then make the unpleasant ones obsolete.

CHAPTER SIX

Fixing the System

When people cannot find a loved one, the person is, indeed, "missing." But, in terms of the law and its practicalities, this reality is complicated by American civil rights and, specifically, our right to privacy. The fact is that *every adult* has the right to disappear. Still, our police and other public servants must "protect and defend" those who are missing and endangered.

It is true that some law enforcement agencies hesitate to assume the responsibility for a missing persons case because, often, the person is voluntarily missing and does not want to be found and, on the other hand, missing persons investigations can be expensive and time consuming. In addition, in many operations, the right hand doesn't know what the left hand is doing. We cannot allow this to occur.

In Tanya's case, the guidelines and their implementation were at fault. In order to save lives, we need to change law enforcement protocols. Only by the grace of God—and good Honda airbags—did Tanya survive for eight days while one-size-fits-all procedures kept her trapped.

While Tanya's accident, her captivity and abandonment in the car, and the aftermath of her ordeal have been devastating, the Riders are determined to turn the entire experience into a positive scenario. They do not want anyone else to have to suffer, clinging to life as Tanya did for more than a week without food, water or medical help.

Fixing the System: Missing Persons Protocol

As a result of their ordeal, Tom and Tanya Rider want to effect change regarding the laws and systems for the handling of missing persons cases. Tom feels that the problem in Tanya's case was that the police departments relied on "cookie cutter" laws. The agencies that Tom contacted tried to fit Tanya's situation into a one-size-fits-all procedure, applying the precedents of "routine" situations to every situation, including Tanya's. This, he feels was a recipe for disaster and, indeed, it proved to be disastrous in Tanya's unique set of circumstances.

The fact is that, when a person is missing, time is critical. Lives are hanging in the balance. To protect everyone, police departments should immediately start investigating upon receiving a 911 call that reports a friend, roommate or family member as "missing." It is also a fact that some of these "missing persons" may have wanted to disappear. Or, they may have been irresponsible—going on vacation without telling anyone or going off on a drunken binge. Yes, it is a fact that police officers and their departments could waste significant and valuable time and resources looking for people who do not want to be found—a wayward boyfriend who escaped to a bar for the night or a long-lost sister who disowned her family and didn't want to tell them that that's what she was doing. Complicating this picture, police must protect the privacy and safety of those wishing to leave abusive situations.

When Tom tried repeatedly to report his wife missing—and then begged the detectives to investigate—Tanya languished in her car, with tragic injuries. When investigators finally suspected that something was amiss, they looked to Tom as the perpetrator of foul play and only then did they begin to launch a proper search investigation. According to Tom, it was a rogue officer who broke department protocol, formed a search-and-rescue search party, and cordoned off the area in question. Were it not for that officer, Tanya very well may have died. Indeed, the hospital doctors said that, had another hour elapsed, she probably wouldn't have made it.

Activism

Today, we have amazing tools at our disposal, including cell phone technology that can "ping" a missing person's cell phone in order to locate it. Unfortunately, it's not always possible to utilize these tools and, further, the right to privacy impedes law enforcement's use of such tools. We need to work to change procedure in this area. First, we need to ensure that our police departments have the immediate authority and responsibility to determine the location of cell phones and to conduct a welfare check so that they can simply tell a searching loved one that the missing person is fine, perhaps adding that the person wished to remain "missing."

Beyond that, police departments, missing person advocates, and the American public should explore forming agreements with all major cell phone service providers, allowing cell phone owners to provide consent that their spouse or any designated loved one(s) may access information regarding the phone's whereabouts. If a person wants to disappear, they can always revoke this permission so that their information remains confidential and their privacy is protected. It is likely that, given the option, most cautious people would gladly give their spouse or parent the ability to find them—and save their lives—if they are mysteriously missing.

Many of the national and state organizations that help to find missing persons and that provide support for their loved ones also advocate for changes in the laws around law enforcement protections of the innocent, as well as laws to keep predators off the street.

The following organizations are very active in affecting change:

Association of Missing and Exploited Children's Organization (AMECO)
703-838-8379 | Toll Free: 877-263-2620
www.amecoinc.org
info@amecoinc.org
An organization of member organizations that provide prevention programs and educational materials.

Polly Klaas Foundation
Hotline: 800-587-4357
www.pollyklaas.org
service@pollyklaas.org
Nonprofit that helps find missing children, works to prevent children from going missing, and promotes laws to help keep children safe.

The Laura Recovery Center
281-482-LRCF(5723) | Toll Free: 866-898-5723
www.lrcf.org
Works to promote education and prevention and provides search services.

In order to change the procedures and protocols of the involved entities, we must first understand the complexities of the issue from the various perspectives: law enforcement, loved ones and, above all, the missing. Then, we will be ready to start a national dialogue on how we can respect the rights of the individual while protecting our loved ones from the type of suffering Tanya Rider endured—whether they are abducted or their car skids off a road into a canal or a ravine. Lives are at stake. The reality is tragic and the cost is great.

"Day to day, we can only do our best with what is served up to us. But, now, I know that—whatever life throws at us—each of us has it within ourselves to conquer all. This strength doesn't belong to me, alone. Rather, each of us must determine that we will overcome the obstacles that come before us."

—Tanya Rider

EPILOGUE

Angels, Eagles and Indomitable Spirit
By Carole Lieberman, M.D.

"I've had a tough angel looking out for me, ever since I was young," Tanya explains with stunning simplicity, when asked about her miraculous survival. Yet, anyone who has learned of her story can't help wanting to know more.

What's a nice girl like you doing in a ravine like this?

Whatever else may have happened that fateful fall day, it must first be understood that Tanya was not familiar with the road she was driving, because she and Tom had just moved to Maple Valley. Yet, she had already decided that she did not feel comfortable on that portion of Highway 169. People were often talking on their cell phones while driving, pieces of wood were hanging out of their trucks and aggressive drivers were cutting people off. "You have to collide together into one lane, so it is emotionally hard for me…. But, I don't take the easy roads." Indeed, metaphorically speaking, Tanya's life has always been a rough road.

What happened in that split second before her car left Highway 169 and plunged into a ravine is still a mystery. It may have been something mundane, like swerving to avoid hitting an animal that was crossing the road.

Or, it may have been the exhausting pursuit of the American Dream that took its toll. They'd just bought land on which to build a dream home, were about to sign a mortgage for the new home they'd barely begun living in, and were paying off a loan for an SUV that still had 'new car smell' in it. Working hard to enjoy the life they'd aspired to, they each took two jobs, sacrificing sleep in the process. Tom worked as a superintendent for SoundBuilt Homes during the day and delivered pizza at night. Tanya worked at the Nordstrom Rack, as a dressing room attendant, from two to ten PM, and at Fred Meyer, stocking health and beauty aids, from midnight to eight AM.

Driving home from Fred Meyer, she may have been too tired to steer well. Fatigue may have caused her eyes to play tricks on her. Or, she may even have fallen asleep at the wheel. "If I was tired, I might've thought of opening the window," Tanya vaguely recalls.

As a little girl, she had learned a painful lesson: Whenever you get something good, you court danger and punishment. Though Tanya acknowledges having had depression since childhood, she's tried hard to break the cycle of her family history. "I've always thought about the brighter picture," she asserts, adding that "people choose to drown out hurtful areas of their lives—in alcohol, relationships, sex.... People make bad choices when they've had bad things happen to them, or bad parents or depression."

Tom and Tanya's anniversary was only a couple of weeks away. Anniversaries are always a time for couples to take stock of their marriage. Although they were in love, their relationship had had its ups and downs. They'd sometimes fight. Their last contact—a telephone conversation—was brief because Tom had told her, in a funny little boy voice, that he was sleeping. She had hung up quickly. Tossing it off, she said that she would hang up on Tom "all the time.... It's part of my charm. I'm angry at my husband 99.9% of the time because men aren't sensitive to women's emotions."

During our sessions of guided imagery, where Tanya was led into a dreamlike-state, her visualizations were relentlessly filled with images of Jeeps. It is possible that a Jeep was coming towards her that day from the opposite direction. Perhaps it was driving over the line and Tanya swerved to avoid a head-on collision. Or perhaps there was foul play, and a Jeep followed her and purposely ran her off the road. In one of her guided-imagery sessions, in which Tanya was asked to visualize herself heading towards the ravine, she saw a disturbing image of a silver-gray Jeep in the parking lot at Fred Meyer. "I try to put myself where I park—a Jeep pops up!" And, indeed, the still shot from Fred Meyer's surveillance camera reveals a chilling picture: a silver gray Jeep parked near Tanya's car the morning she was last seen.

There may have been other types of foul play afoot. For example, someone may have tampered with Tanya's car. Tom told the detective that, about a week before she disappeared, Tanya had called him from her work at the Nordstrom Rack. She was distraught. "She'd called up and was asking, 'Why are all these people laughing at... me?' 'I don't know, hon. I'm not there. What's going on?' And she just said, 'Well, these people keep walking by my car, and they're laughing'. I said, 'Well, hon, maybe, maybe they're not laughing at you'. That's part of her depression... she thinks everything's aimed at her.... She said a few of 'em were just customers and then one of 'em was a girl who'd been snotty with her at the ... Nordstrom Rack."

Why and how Tanya ended up in a ravine off Highway 169 is still an unsolved mystery. But, what is clear is that the Sheriff's Department spent more time suspecting Tom of domestic violence and investigating him than they did looking for her. From the beginning, the detective told him, "A lot of times what happens is ... people just need a break. For whatever reason, they're just gone for a time.... The spouse of a missing person (is) typically somebody law enforcement has to clear ... because ... statistically if something bad is gonna happen to a person, it's gonna be with somebody they know.... Any domestic violence history between you guys?" Tom tried to assure him, "I've never raised a hand to her."

A deputy wrote that Tom "said he doesn't want KCSO [King County Sheriff's Office] to bother getting any warrants to search anything, that he will give access to anything detectives want." Tom "said he is concerned they will spend time trying to eliminate him as a suspect, instead of trying to locate victim." And he was right. Ironically, eight days later, as Tom had begun taking their polygraph test, Tanya was finally found. If Sheriffs would have searched for Tanya sooner, she could have been spared some of the trauma of being trapped. And there still would have been time enough to arrest Tom and put him in jail, if her condition validated their suspicions.

Asking Tanya, "What's a nice girl like you doing in a ravine like this?" does not solve the mystery. When confronted with continuing speculation, Tanya's response most often is, "My mind has chosen to forget how I got into the ravine. This way, I have peace." But it is only an illusion of peace. Repressing memories of eight days of trauma takes its toll.

The Lost Eight Days

Ironically, while Tanya was buried in blackberry bushes, Tom was at work clearing blackberry bushes from a different wood, when he got the call that she was missing.

At the beginning, Tanya held on to hope that she would be rescued, just as she had held on to hope of her father rescuing her when she was a little girl. But her childhood dreams had been dashed, as he never did come riding in on a white horse to save her.

Andrew Lloyd Webber's song "Memory," from the musical *Cats*, could well have served as the backdrop to Tanya's entrapment.

Epilogue

Daylight, see the dew on the sunflower
And a rose that is fading
Roses wither away
Like the sunflower I yearn to turn my face to the dawn
I am waiting for the day.

While she was waiting, Tanya desperately longed for her deceased dog, Lady, who had comforted her countless times in the past.

Through guided-imagery sessions, where Tanya was soothed into deep relaxation and an altered state of consciousness, she was able to see flashes of visual images from these lost eight days. "I didn't know where I was.... I couldn't see cars. I could only hear them.... I knocked on the window a lot, hoping someone would hear me.... I tugged at my seat belt. It wouldn't come off.... The music was on. I turned it up real loud.... Why hadn't I bought seat belt covers? I wish I had.... I can't get my seat belt off. It's irritating me!"

Tanya pulled her phone from the dashboard, through the steering wheel, to call 911. At least, this is what she imagined she was doing. In actuality, Tanya couldn't reach her phone. After she was rescued, Tanya adamantly insisted that she'd called 911 and had told the police that she had gone off the road and needed help. But, in her mind, they had only laughed at her and called her "stupid." She also believed she had called Tom and was furious with him for taking so long to get to her. It may have been wish-fulfillment dreams, hallucinations or delusions. But, there were no records of these calls. On the other hand, many people did try calling her, to no avail. In her guided image she saw, "My phone is somewhere over there. I can't reach it. I hear it ringing."

While trapped, as Tanya became hungry and thirsty, she thought of having stopped at Whole Foods earlier that morning, after having gotten off work. When she was brought back to these moments, through her guided images, she recalled, "I felt gross stopping at Whole Foods because I'd just gotten off my dirty job, where I'm on my knees a lot. Around this time, somebody spilled Scope on the floor and I got some on the bottom of my foot.... I used to like to get pancakes at Whole Foods, but I go with what my body's craving.... I bought bottled water. Water is my first priority.... When I would come back home, I would crash. So, I would get something to eat that I'd eat later, when I woke up. We didn't have a fridge here.... There was something I was getting that I liked. I used to make salads in their deli bar. I don't know if I did that that day. I liked the scrambled eggs and I sprinkled cheese on top.... I don't have a recollection of eating or drinking anything that day."

Tanya's pleasant imagery of her favorite foods was suddenly interrupted by her recall of a "foul smell." "I'm thinking I'm never gonna buy that again." But, what Tanya had thought was bad food, was actually her bodily wastes. She recalls that, again and again, "I had to go to the bathroom in my seat and I was crying." Since she was not able to eat or drink, her body began essentially 'eating' and 'drinking' itself— producing urine and feces that piled up around her. This was agonizing for Tanya, who had long striven for order and cleanliness.

> *Memory, all alone in the moonlight*
> *I can smile at the old days*
> *I was beautiful then*
> *I remember the time I knew what happiness was*
> *Let the memory live again.*

As each day passed, Tanya's life became more surreal. She floated in and out of consciousness. Except for the searing pain, it was akin to being in a sensory-deprivation tank. And while her body was shutting down, she was fighting thoughts that she was going to die. "There was no way I could have survived eight days without God. God's taken away my memories.... But my body remembers.... The evidence is written in my scars."

Indeed, the universe brought many forces together to save Tanya. During all the years she'd tried to ward off depression, by focusing on her health, she'd obsessively worked out at the gym, done other exercises, eaten health food, and taken herbs and natural dietary supplements. So, her body was in good shape. The dogged discipline she'd honed in order to persevere with her health regimen helped her persevere in her fight for survival.

Though Tanya's body was trapped, her mind wasn't. Because of her abusive childhood, she had learned to disconnect herself from her body and her surroundings. This time, once again, the protective psychological mechanism of dissociation would save her from entrapment. She was able to rise above her physical self and float off to a happier, prettier place, instead of the desperate situation in which she was trapped. Tanya has said that, while she was pinned behind the wheel, it felt as though her beloved dog, Lady, was taking her on a sightseeing tour, guiding her away from misery to more serene settings, like ethereal Thomas Kincaid paintings of idyllic landscapes bathed in light.

Tanya's determination also saved her. Her mantra, in defiance of her abusive childhood, had long been "I will not be anybody's victim." When asked what she thought about in order to not give up, Tanya said, "Tom and I—our love is not breakable." And, "If you have a deep relationship with God, it's not breakable."

> *Daylight, I must wait for the sunrise*
> *I must think of a new life*
> *And I mustn't give in*
> *When the dawn comes tonight will be a memory too*
> *And a new day will begin.*

When Tanya was found, on the same day that she and Tom were

supposed to put their final signatures on their mortgage papers, she was hanging from her seatbelt. "When the police officer crashed his way through my car window on the passenger side, it startled me. I was very scared of him.... And he was stunned because I was able to talk to him and drink water."

Miracle of Maple Valley

Though Tanya is not the first, nor only, one to survive without food or water for more than a week, it is still unusual. Some might even say it is a miracle.

Before Tanya could be extricated from her crushed and mangled SUV, she anxiously told the medics who arrived on the scene, "I can't feel my legs." Tanya was bewildered and covered in diffuse glass fragments from her windshield. It took over two hours to disentangle her from the wreckage, during which time her breathing slowed and almost stopped, prompting the medics to intubate her. According to the medical records, they were "unable to get a pulse, so a trauma code was called."

When Airlift Northwest transported her from the scene to Harborview Medical Center, they noted that Tanya had a "laceration above left eye.... Bruising from left shoulder to right pelvis—appears to follow seat belt line." Her lungs had "breath sounds" that were "diminished." They observed skin "breakdown" into "decubitus" ulcers from prolonged pressure over her pelvis and knees. They also diagnosed her as having a head injury, abdominal injury, multiple trauma, and hypovolemia (a decrease in the volume of circulating blood).

When Tanya got to Harborview Medical Center, emergency room doctors rushed to stabilize her. They intensively infused fluid close to her heart and performed the most urgent diagnostic tests. Before she left the ER, her list of diagnoses had lengthened: threatened limbs—both legs were without a pulse; pressure ulcers on her pelvis, both legs, and abdomen where the seat belt was; fractures of her ribs, left clavicle, and a spinal vertebra; acute kidney failure; pneumomediastinum (air in the middle of the chest due to leaks from the lungs or airways); pneumoretroperitoneum (air behind the lining of the abdominal cavity); and pockets of air in her right armpit.

Tanya was taken for x-rays and CAT scans and then transferred straight to the Intensive Care Unit. "Initially, she was awake and following commands." But this didn't last long. Since her body temperature was only 87.6 degrees Fahrenheit instead of the normal 98.6, doctors initiated "aggressive rewarming." Blood test results indicated that she had hypernatremia (too much sodium in the blood); acidosis (too much acid in the blood); and rhabdomyolysis (the breakdown of muscles, releasing muscle fiber contents into the blood and causing kidney damage). Her left shoulder was dislocated. Her left forehead laceration cut through her left eyebrow, and the connective tissue sheath covering her bone was exposed. Deep patches of dead skin dotted her chest, abdomen, left elbow and both hips and legs.

It soon became apparent that her left leg had developed 'compartment syndrome,' because the muscles, nerves and blood vessels had been compressed for too long. In an effort to save her leg, Tanya was rushed to the operating room for an emergency left leg fasciotomy, the cutting away of the connective tissue covering her muscles, to relieve the pressure.

During the first week, Tanya was in a medically induced coma and on a respirator. Meanwhile, caring citizens went to the site of her accident and searched for things that may have inadvertently been left in the ravine. They retrieved her social security card, the book that contained plans for the house she and Tom were building, and more items, which they returned to her.

Tanya's first memory in the hospital was becoming "aware of lots of people around me, fiddling around my legs. I asked the nurse for something to drink. She said, 'We have juice'." Somewhat disoriented, unable to comprehend the seriousness of her situation and locked into her dietary prohibitions, Tanya asked her if there was sugar in it. "We have water," the nurse replied. When Tanya innocently inquired, "Bottled?" the nurse looked at her in disbelief. "I was hungry, too," Tanya added. "I also remember a nurse trying to get out of me what happened. 'Did you fall asleep?' she asked. I don't know."

When she questioned Tom about what happened, at first, he told her not to worry and said that she was a "miracle." Tanya didn't understand. He told her more, a little bit at a time, stopping when he thought it was too much for her. "You were lost for awhile and then we found you," he added later. Tom brought her the cell phone she had had in the car. "I kept it under my pillow so I could call him."

When Tanya saw her mother walking towards her bed, her first thoughts were, "She's my abuser. I can't move. I was shocked she was there. She pushed her way in even though she knew I didn't want her there. She wasn't being mean, so I let her come back and try to be helpful…. I was on a lot of drugs, so I let things happen I didn't want."

After the first week, Tanya was transferred out of ICU and into a regular room. Tanya recollects "a police officer at my bedside, a man with black hair. He said, 'I'm the one who rescued you.' I felt gratitude towards him, but he didn't seem to accept my gratitude. He was staring at me with no emotion. He said that there were a lot of people involved. I said, 'God.' He asked me what I remembered. He said, 'We tore the roof off your car. You don't remember that?' I said, 'It was so nice of you to stop by and see me.' He said, 'I was just here doing something else.' It was weird."

A rehabilitation psychologist noted that Tanya "had a vivid and apparently accurate recall for the accident." But two days later, curiously, things changed. "Today, the patient denies recollection of the accident and the period of time she was trapped in the car.... Patient's husband is now happy that patient does not recall the event. He is concerned about his wife's well being should those memories return."

Two days after this, the rehab psychologist noted, "Patient reports two nightmares.... She states that she wakes in fear but then falls back to sleep and does not remember their content.... Patient continues to deny memories of event and she states she is happy about the lack of memories." A couple of weeks later, he wrote, "Patient continues to deny recollection of event.... She is able to recount the story again based on what she has been told without... apparent distress." Yet, subsequently, Tanya has locked these memories away.

When Tanya first saw one of her wounds, as the nurse started to change the dressing, she became frantic. "I asked the nurse for a washcloth to put over my eyes. After that, I didn't let them let me see it. I had them cover my eyes so I couldn't see my wounds." Indeed, this was a concrete symbol of what Tanya has been doing all of her life. Just as she has done with her emotional wounds from childhood and her accident, she blocks out memories so that she won't have to "see" what really happened.

Tanya dreaded the painful, twice-daily wound changes. She "howled," like her dog Lady, hoping it would be as soothing to her as it had seemed to be for Lady. But Tanya dreaded looking at her emotional wounds even more, terrified that they would cause more pain than howling or painkillers could muffle.

After she was at Harborview for almost a month, the surgery team asked the Psychiatry Consultation and Liaison Service to evaluate Tanya for anxiety and depression. By this point, she had had three more surgeries on her leg, another surgery to repair her clavicle fracture, and another to close her facial laceration. The psychiatrist wrote that Tanya "does not have any memory about events leading to the car accident.... She apparently did not know about the extensive media coverage regarding her case until recently.... Her husband... has appeared on many media outlets. Several days ago he brought a DVD recapping some of the media coverage... and they watched this video together. She describes this as being incredibly sad, but at the same time quite incredible (which reinforced her belief of the amazing power of God). She feels incredibly blessed to be alive and believes that God has been playing a large part in her survival and recovery."

After almost a month, Tanya "stood for the first time." The rehab psychologist noted that she had "less of a vacant gaze." She had been having problems with her appetite, since the beginning of her hospitalization. Hospital records described her as "emaciated." Tanya recalls fondly that, "the nutritionist came into play. She helped me with my need to eat healthy foods. She got them to bring organic salads and for the cook to make me brown rice and eggs. My husband brought me food. And I drank a lot of Ensure."

About six weeks into her stay, the rehab psychologist observed Tanya to be "crying uncontrollably" and "frustrated with (the) need for additional surgeries." An anesthesiologist had told her, "You're the star here in Seattle," but it hadn't seemed to help. Instead, Tanya said, "I'm feeling really sad right now. I want to be done with this and go home."

Tanya had been trying to sit up. "I don't remember how I got up. My heart got used to lying down. I thought I'd throw up when I sat up. I couldn't sit up very long, so they put me down again." When she was able to sit up she realized, "I had a beautiful view. There was life happening in Seattle. I felt so far away from being a productive citizen."

After about seven weeks, though Tanya had worked with other physical therapists, she refused to work with one of them, with whom she felt unsafe. Tanya became anxious that she would fall. She tried harder, though she still had bad days.

A teaching hospital, Harborview is staffed by doctors and residents from the University of Washington. Groups of them visited Tanya on daily rounds. One day, "I asked a woman resident, 'Am I going to walk again?' She looked at me with so much hope, and said, 'You will walk again'." But one of the supervising doctors pulled the resident away, dashing Tanya's hopes with, "There's no guarantee of that."

Two months into her hospital stay, despite ongoing surgical procedures, Tanya was able to stand and transfer into a wheelchair with minimal assistance.

She'd gone from lying down to sitting up, to getting out of bed and into a wheelchair, and later to a walker. "It was like the two-hour workout I used to do at the gym—just getting to the bed or to the potty. Many times, I almost fell backwards. It was really traumatic to realize I didn't have control of my body."

Soon it would be decided whether Tanya would transfer to inpatient rehabilitation, where she could progress at a more accelerated pace, or to a skilled nursing facility, where there would be little expectation of progress. In order to be eligible for inpatient rehab, she would have to reach certain milestones of mobility. This was proving difficult for her because of her "anxiety and difficulty trusting." Tanya had refused to take an antidepressant when it was recommended weeks before, but "bouts of tearfulness" had persisted. And, now, she needed to overcome the fears that were holding her back—before her fate was decided for her. Since the doctors would not agree to let her take her natural supplements, Tanya finally agreed to take an antidepressant (all the while, promising herself that she would resume her nutritional approach as soon as she returned home).

"The physical therapist said, 'You either walk or you go to a nursing home.' In order to go to rehab, I had to show that I could do many tasks. I had to do a lot of exercises with my hands and feet in bed. I had to be able to sit up for a long amount of time. It was making me dizzy and I had no cushion on my bottom, because I had no more fat or muscle there, so it was painful. I got that rubbing thing on my bottom bone—bedsores—

so I had to move around."

Tanya's chances were not looking good. But, when the rehabilitation medicine doctor rejected her for the inpatient unit, Tanya dug down deeper. "I was gonna get out of that victim state! But I only had a short time to go from the wheelchair to the walker." Determined to show them that she could do it, Tanya made enough progress to be admitted to rehab less than a week later. It was the beginning of December, and she told them her goal was to be discharged home by Christmas.

"I was so happy I got into rehab! I liked the painted butterflies on the ceiling. I could see the light. Soon, I'd be going home." Tanya's mother visited her there, and chirped, "Your doctor said you're a go-getter. You'll be leaving soon." But, when she saw Tanya was sullen, Nancy asked, "Do you want me to leave?"

"I said, 'Yes.' I made sure my mother, grandmother, and uncle couldn't get in to see me. My grandmother never has nice things to say. She said, 'Tanya looks really thin.' They were looking at me like I'm a freak." Although Tanya was desperate to see love in their eyes, especially at this vulnerable time, all she saw was judgment.

Once Tanya was on the rehab unit, she was seen by more rehab psychologists. They noted that Tanya's physical therapists "report that while patient is participating in therapies, she is highly anxious and micro-manages therapeutic sessions. These behaviors are pre-morbid in nature," (meaning that her behaviors were personality traits that pre-existed her current medical problems). She was still "very fearful of falling." A week later, Tanya listed her accomplishments: "increased appetite, increased endurance, a successful trip to the health food store… walking up and down four stairs." The staff commented, "Patient did note difficulty being in a crowd at the store, but believes she was able to handle it adequately."

The day before her discharge, Tanya went on an outing and "got her hair detangled." The accident had wreaked havoc with it. In fact, since the accident, for several reasons, she'd felt that she had "no femininity."

Epilogue

Tom bought Tanya a pretty workout outfit to wear when she went home from the hospital. He bought black bell-bottom pants that could fit over her bandages, and a fancy black top with gemstones sewn in, with a large v-neck that would make it easier to put on.

Finally, on December 21, 2007, after a three-month stay, Tanya was discharged from Harborview. She had reached her goal of being home by Christmas! Her discharge diagnoses were listed as: polytrauma with multiple wounds; shoulder dislocation; left radial nerve palsy (wrist drop); left foot drop; deep vein thrombosis; anxiety; depression; and pain management. She was discharged on twelve different medications, including "significant amounts of pain medication" and the antidepressant.

By discharge, Tanya had progressed to being able to walk household distances with supervision and a cane. She could independently move from a sitting position to a standing one, and go up and down stairs if assistance was nearby. She could partially dress herself and could prepare a light meal, but she could not go back to work yet. She still needed a visiting nurse as well as physical and occupational therapy. Her wounds still needed cleansing and dressing. And she would have to make an endless stream of doctor visits.

When Tanya came home from the hospital, these worries dissipated upon seeing the snowwoman Tom had made in their front yard. It made her smile. And something else made her smile even wider. "Tom said that, when I woke up in the hospital, I asked him where my Honda Element was. He knows how hard it is for me to buy good things for myself. Tom asked what kind of car I wanted. I said I wanted the same car. Before I got home, he bought a new blue Element—one year newer than my last one. We kept the same name for the car, Skywalker. I name cars because they're part of the family, and they get me away from things." Indeed, one would think that the last car that Tanya would want would be the same car that had trapped her. Perhaps it can be attributed to an idiosyncratic form of Stockholm Syndrome, where Tanya fell in love with her captor—a blue

Honda Element.

Although she was smiling when she got home, the cycle of sleep-pain-wound-change, sleep-pain-wound-change, sleep-pain-wound-change that had droned on throughout her hospital stay like a broken record, was not over.

A month later, Tom accompanied Tanya when she was seen in the Rehab Clinic. She "appeared anxious and irritable… fearful, jumpy." Although she was gradually progressing physically, she was not doing as well psychologically. The nurse practitioner wrote, "She stays home by herself during the day when her husband goes to work." Tanya reported "Occasional night dreams…. She gets pretty drenched with sweat…. She does not want her husband driving too close to another car, as she is 'not comfortable.'"

During her wound-care appointments, Tanya was referred to an outpatient rehab psychologist, who wrote in the progress notes that Tanya "complains of nightmares that… leave her with a funny feeling…. She is currently pondering the meaning of this accident and is grateful she is alive." She also "emphasized that she is fortunate that the 'love of her life' still finds her attractive and, therefore, she is not concerned about her appearance."

Less than nine months after the accident, Tanya was able to walk without a cane and had begun to drive. But her injuries, especially the open wound on her left hip and thigh, still necessitated treatment.

The rehab psychologist wrote that Tanya "has been in and out of the hospital" since she was originally discharged. "Pain is especially bad since she has returned to work and is on her feet." Tanya had returned to work at Nordstrom in December 2008, fifteen months after the accident. Though she continues to be plagued by wound infections, pain and other problems, she is still grateful to be alive.

Epilogue

Road to Recovery

Now, Tanya is heading down another road—the road to recovery, which has as many twists, turns and precarious spots as Highway 169. She has both physical and psychological injuries from which to recover. The scars from her physical wounds are more apparent. But the psychological scars are deeper and more painful, which is why Tanya doesn't want to remember them.

"I'm not gonna remember those eight days. I'm gonna set the line.... I look at what happened to me down there as evil. Evil can take control of me. I don't like anything to control me."

Untangling the origin of Tanya's memory loss is a complicated affair. Part of it may be traced to traumatic amnesia. This could have happened as a result of brain injury from the concussive force of impact of the accident, or as a result of changes in the brain that caused a disruption of its memory circuits while Tanya languished in the ravine.

Undoubtedly, her psyche is repressing painful memories and perpetually pushing them down into her unconscious, as a psychological defense mechanism. But, certainly, by her own admission, a significant part of her memory loss is willful, conscious 'forgetting' because she simply doesn't *want* to remember. This is also evidenced by her spurious memory lapses. Since the accident, she has at times spoken of her recollections and, at other times, denied recollecting anything.

Interestingly, when Tom was asked why he hasn't been curious enough about these lost memories to persuade Tanya to remember more, he said, "No. I've wanted to stay sane and not choke the police officer. Tanya isn't ready. I'll be glad if she never remembers."

Tanya's memory of the last time she saw Tom before the accident is "blurry." "I saw Tom at night. I think he was bringing me food." This may be an actual recall or it may be a wish-fulfillment fantasy. As a child,

Tanya was starved of food and of the love it represents. Her attempts to eat food that's healthy and good for her has become a way that she tries to show love to herself. Being trapped in her car, and starving, was all the more traumatic because it recapitulated being a prisoner in her mother's home, where the cupboards were bare.

Tanya's cars had always been sanctuaries for her, places where she could get away, be alone and have peace. "I come to my car on my lunch break. It helps me get sane so I can go back to my job." Imagine, then, how disturbing it was to feel her sanctuary filling up with urine and feces. This was all that much harder because of Tanya's obsessive-compulsive traits. Her menacing and out-of-control childhood instilled in Tanya a need to be in control of her body, her surroundings and her life, lest she be harmed again by some danger lurking in the shadows.

Being trapped in such a small space has made Tanya claustrophobic. "I don't like sitting in doctors' waiting rooms. I have to go out. Flying is an issue for me because you have to sit in a confined space for a long period of time."

A big part of Tanya's recovery consists of her trying to let go of anger, especially towards the Sheriff's Department that delayed looking for her. "It's like they were saying, 'You don't deserve to be found. If you're a purse, we'll take a report. We don't want to look for working people.' But Tom and I paid a lot of money to King County for our house.... My husband took me away from my abusers. They think he's an abuser. Tom could have become the next 'Fugitive'."

After Tanya's story hit the news and Tom posted a reward, people came forward with information. "A man said he'd gone to the Fire Department and told them that 'the road didn't look right. It looked like someone went off it.' Later, the Fire Department said they'd searched the wrong place.... People told my husband that others have gone off the road there. After my accident, they filled the hole in and put a guardrail."

Amongst the complex emotions Tanya is feeling is depression, which is anger directed inward towards the self. She has struggled with depression throughout her life and, now, it is heightened. She takes supplements like kava kava, ginseng, St. John's wort and coconut water. "You need to focus on what makes you happy to fight depression," she believes. "Sometimes, it's a nice salmon dinner with Omega-3 fatty acids. Sometimes it's B vitamins, having Tom make me laugh, eating health food or getting exercise."

"If you end your life, you go to hell," Tanya asserts. "I have never thought of killing myself. I've thought life is really hard. Never wished I was dead. I've always known God has a purpose…. Anyway, according to King County's strict criteria, if I was suicidal they should have looked for me!"

It has long been important to Tanya to feel attractive. The accident not only wrecked her car and her body, but also her self-image and self-esteem. It has left her feeling damaged. In the hospital, Tanya hadn't wanted to see herself in the mirror. To this day, when reflecting upon her traumatic experience, Tanya gets a 'deer caught in headlights' look. But there is also something very spiritual about her, as if she's seen something mysterious and otherworldly.

When Tanya was found, her "fingernails and toenails were yellow from malnutrition." Her knuckles had "big monstrous" black scabs on them. But this was the least of it. She still has wounds on her body that haven't yet healed and she has been left with a scar on her forehead. "When I worked at night, I wore glasses. I have a gouge in my head. We think the airbag crushed my glasses into my forehead." Each morning, Tanya painstakingly styles her hair in a manner that will hide the scar.

Tanya eventually returned to work at Nordstrom's. "I was feeling disabled at my job. I had to walk around every hour. I missed days of work and I was late because my injuries are painful. I had to wear two wrist braces at work for a while. My coworkers asked about it." Most recently, after her leg wound reopened, Tanya's infectious disease doctor put her on disability, so that she could rest, "to try to stop my leg from continuing to get infected.... I'm not gonna be in a victim state."

Tanya and Tom were two lost souls who found each other, until one of them got lost again. Not only was Tanya lost, but her engagement and wedding rings were also lost somewhere in the wreckage. Tom has told her that their dog, Sheba, ate his wedding ring when she was a puppy.

Tanya tearfully admits, "We haven't been intimate since my accident. Tom's afraid he's going to hurt me. He sees I'm in pain. There's a lot of 'ow, ow, ow.'"

Tom agrees that he doesn't want to hurt Tanya by having sex with her. "When we get into position and she says, 'Ow,' I lose my erection." He also describes their lack of intimacy from a slightly different perspective. "I have a mental block when it comes to sex, from having to dress my wife's wounds twice a day. I was the only one she would allow to roll her on her side. When she came home from the hospital, she couldn't reach her wounds. Her left wrist and ankle were paralyzed. And she didn't want to look at them."

This put Tom into a 'care-giving role,' which unconsciously reminded him of having to be a caregiver to his mom when she was drunk. It is natural for a man to be unable to have sex with a woman who reminds him of the taboo against having sex with his mother. To complicate the situation further, Tom, as a little boy, had been helpless to protect his mother from all of the abuse she received from men. Now, since he was helpless to protect Tanya from languishing in the ravine, it has triggered these memories and made him feel like less of a man.

The lost eight days have also interfered with their plans to have children. Tanya explains, "My husband is very passionate about having kids. I didn't want to have children and hurt them like my parents did. I don't want to be like my parents. I always said, 'When we have a house, we'll have children.'" The sad irony is that, now they have a house, but they are having problems with sexual intimacy.

"It's very hard. But it's not breaking us up. I know he's into me…. I had no self- esteem when I met Tom. He's told me for eighteen years that I'm beautiful and I'm his princess…. In the hospital, I had dreadlocks, no bottom, no chest, no femininity. That's when he would've left me. But our love survived."

Memories: Setting Tanya Free

Touch me, it's so easy to leave me
All alone with the memory
Of my days in the sun
If you touch me you'll understand what happiness is
Look, a new day has begun.

Tanya has come forward with her story because "people don't want to believe I survived eight days…. I feel it's my duty to God to let people know about this miracle. Maybe God is leading me to do this, making it my time to shine."

Although Tanya has escaped her childhood prisons, and the cold metal carcass that entombed her in the ravine, she still holds memories of eight days of horror locked deep inside. Has she imprisoned them, or are the memories still holding her captive?

Shepherding Tanya into meditative guided imagery—or waking dreams—seems to be the only way for her to feel safe enough to retrieve fragments of her memories from these lost days. Following the suggestion to visualize herself in a meadow, Tanya saw:

"Blue sky … mountain … butterflies … wind blowing the bushes … bugs flying around me … my bottom half is buried in flowers. It's hard to get up … Blue sky … the white peak of a mountain … I'm in a dark space … I see a field … bluish darker mountains … trees cut on top … mountains are getting darker … white hat on a girl … I'm disconnecting from it … black ribbon around the white hat … girl … no movement in this picture … not cheery … girl … just seeing the back of her head … wind just blew her hair … large wind gust … nothing moving, but wind blowing around girl's hair … wildlife … I'm afraid of snakes … not safe."

Epilogue

To help her move through this scary part and to continue her reverie, Tanya was asked to visualize herself in the safest place she's ever known. Under her breath she said, "I never had a safe place."

Soon Tanya returned to the meadow-like ravine, where she saw:

> *"Shadows of the sun on a tree ... the tree grows dark."* She then began seeing *"things that that resemble things on the side of the road ... black and white square ... yield sign ... stake like in the ground ... yellow and black bars ... road signs in the way ... the light thing that hangs down at the intersection—yellow, red, green, hanging over the road ... red, yellow, green ... they're not lit ... one-way sign ... a seagull on top of the light ... a car with headlights on ... Jeep ... Why is everything rolling around? ... crying noises ... man with brown hair, black sunglasses, rainbow colors on his t-shirt ... laughing, looks upset ... road signs ... black and white markers ... yellow and white."*

Here, Tanya started breathing hard and holding her neck as if in pain. She covered her face and rubbed her painful left wrist.

> *"Rocks in road in front ... there was green grass ... it became dead grass ... it's paved ... the road is changing ... round rocks, big, solid, now sharper rocks ... Washington state highway sign with a green background and a picture of Washington ... shadow of something on the pavement ... I'm on the road ... looking at the road ... Lady smiling. Lady has a cute smile, white teeth ... blue flashes of color of my car ... Washington license plate ... Lady is my dog ... I keep seeing black and the hood of my car ... confused ... white car in and out, in and out ... house has a dome roof like the top of a cathedral ... trees ... like I'm floating ... I went in the cathedral ... the sky is so pretty ... the top of the cathedral*

*is golden ... sunset ... dark orange, yellow ... look at the water
... the horizon ... waves ... I see the black part of my car ... the
driver's inside molding of the window ... I have Lady. She looks
startled but then she smiled. She's sticking her tongue out. I could
see her teeth. There's the shadow of Lady on the window—or
it's a reflection of her ... We're in a different kind of water with
canyons ... It's dark in the middle ... The sun's hitting the canyon
... Lady's in front, looking out at the scenery ... water with trees,
flat stagnant water ... Now Lady's looking out the front window
... always a pretty picture in the background ... Lady's smiling ...
road ... stagnant water ... Lady turned her head in front of me ...
road went down ... road that has broken off ... running water over
it ... Lady is always right here."* Tanya points to the space in front
of her and on the left, the driver's side.

Once again, visualizing herself in the ravine, Tanya continued:

*"I'm stuck in a sandcastle ... I see a bald eagle sideways. He's
looking at me with yellow-greenish eyes ... I see his head, his beak
... He's white with a little black. But I don't see the rest of him ...
on the road, why are the white lines not together? ... The bald
eagle is very interested in me. He has not left ... I've never been
that close to a bald eagle. He has a white head ... I see his eyes
... The color of the front of my SUV keeps coming. He's on the
edge of my hood ... green in front of me ... the eagle has not left
... There's something dark in front of me. I don't want it to be the
inside of my car ... yellow and orange car controls ... yellow feet
of the eagle. He's trying to keep his grip. Skinny legs ... he seems
more interested in getting off the hood. He's looking down in front
... black-and-white road sign ... Why does he get to hop off the
hood? He's thinking about it ... Now the eagle is not looking at*

me. He's focusing on what's below. I see his back, yellowy legs ... black in front of me ... my vent ... stagnant picture ... I'm trying not to see more ... I see the color of my car, the hood of my car, the eagle, and green in the background."

Here, Tanya started sobbing, as the vision of the eagle—perched on her car hood, keeping her company—came flooding back. She could still see the light shining from within the eagle and radiating outwards. It is her most poignant memory of these lost days. And how profound! The eagle is believed to be the liaison between man and God. For every prayer, an eagle soars inside of us, lifting our prayers to the sky. And, as a messenger of God, the eagle brings us strength, courage, healing, and spiritual protection. How Tanya became trapped in the ravine is still a mystery, but the eagle knows how she survived!

A Final Note for The Reader

As you've read of Tanya's harrowing experiences that culminated in her miraculous survival, you have undoubtedly marveled at the strength of the human spirit. Though none of us sets out in the morning thinking that we will become trapped and missing for eight days, we each have endured or will endure our own traumatic experiences.

What would *you* do if you were suddenly 'trapped' in a decimated car, another type of accident, or a natural or man-made disaster?

Of course, it's best to prepare for such catastrophes before you find yourself ensnared in one. For example, you should build stamina by exercising regularly, eating healthy foods and getting enough sleep. Keep water and energy bars with you. Store safety kits in your car and home. And make sure that at least one person knows where you are at all times, so that, if you seem to be missing, they will know where you're likely to be.

If you do become trapped, here's some psychological advice to help bolster your will to survive.

Never let go of hope. Make a mental list of all the forces that are coming to your rescue, such as people who will notice that you are missing, passersby who have seen the traumatic event, other victims who have managed to escape and will notify the authorities, and so on. Close your eyes and visualize paramedics in ambulances, firefighters in engines, pilots in helicopters—all rushing to your aid.

Then, while you are waiting for them to arrive, visualize yourself in the place that made you feel the safest in your whole life. Perhaps it was snuggled under the covers in your childhood bed with your stuffed animals around you, or lying under a tree in a secret spot in your backyard looking up at the soft, floating clouds. Invite comforting people or pets into your reverie, as well.

Don't wait for your life to pass before you. Concentrate on all the wonderful experiences you have had and recreate them as though you are watching a movie. Remind yourself of all your accomplishments, your travels, your mischief, lovemaking and laughter.

Connect yourself to your loved ones. Tell yourself that you have to hold on for them because of how much they would yearn for you and you for them if you were gone for good. Remind yourself how important you are to the world. You are here for a reason. Have you finished giving all of your gifts to the world? Surely, you have more to give.

Pray. Tragic circumstances can move even the most confirmed atheists to prayer. Connect with your God or Higher Power. Watch for your "eagle" or other sign that the universe has sent to keep you company and reassure you that all will be well.

Hopefully, you will never need to use this advice. But, meanwhile, it behooves each of us to work towards bringing the policies of our local 911 department, Sheriff's department and police department into the twenty-first century. With ever-advancing technology, there are now ways to locate the "missing" much more quickly, while protecting them from people they may have wanted to escape.

Tanya's long road to recovery still stretches out in front of her. Our sessions of guided imagery were only her first step. She needs years—if not a lifetime—of medical treatment and psychotherapy. But, each time her story touches a reader's heart, she will feel a gentle nudge towards her destiny of being healed and whole.

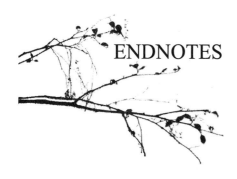

ENDNOTES

Chapter Three

[1] Lewis Kamb, "Without a Trace," *Seattle Post-Intelligencer*, February 17, 2003.

[2] "Remembering Someone Who is Missing," Let's Bring Them Home The National Center for Missing Adults, http://www.theyaremissed. org/ncma/content.php?webid=remembering, accessed on December 20, 2010.

Chapter Five

[1] Friedrich Nietzsche, *Twilight of the Idols*, 1888, "Maxims and Arrows."

[2] Eleanor Roosevelt, *You Learn By Living*, 1960, pp. 29-30.

[3] Khalil Gibran, The Prophet, "On Pain," 1923.

[4] Oprah Winfrey, Commencement Address, Wellesley College, May 30, 1997.

[5] Winston Churchill, "Night Bombing of London: 'Every Man to His Post'" in *Complete Speeches*, vol. 6, 6277.

[6] Winston Churchill, unsourced.

[7] Dr. Seuss, *I Had Trouble in Getting to Solla Sollew*, Collins, 1967.

[8] Ralph Waldo Emerson, unsourced.

[9] J.K. Rowling, "A Sluggish Memory," *Harry Potter and the Half-Blood Prince*, 2006.

[10] Bill Cosby, unsourced.

TRACY C. ERTL

An eighteen-year veteran 911 dispatcher in Green Bay, Wisconsin, Tracy C. Ertl is the publisher of TitleTown Publishing LLC, a vibrant, national house specializing in survival and true crime stories. She is a nationally renowned instructor in active shooter incidents for APCO International, and she writes "Riding the Alligator: Dispatches from the Frontlines of Law Enforcement (and Life)," a dispatch related blog for *Psychology Today*.

Photo by Chuck Leininger.

CAROLE LIEBERMAN, M.D.

Carole Lieberman, M.D. is a Beverly Hills forensic psychiatrist and expert witness who testifies in high-profile trials. She is also a bestselling author and speaker. Her books include *Bad Boys: Why We Love Them, How to Live with Them, and When to Leave Them; Coping with Terrorism: Dreams Interrupted;* and most recently *Bad Girls: Why Men Love Them & How Good Girls Can Learn Their Secrets.*

You will recognize Dr. Carole, a three-time Emmy award-winner, from her countless appearances on TV, including: Oprah, Larry King, O'Reilly, The Today Show, Good Morning America, CNN, Fox News, BBC and many others.

She also hosts "Dr. Carole's Couch," a popular radio talk show, and is quoted in magazines and newspapers around the world.

One of society's most highly respected psychiatrists, Dr. Lieberman is well known for her insight into the social issues of our time, from dating to dealing with the threat of terrorism.

She is a Diplomate of the American Board of Psychiatry and Neurology, and a well-regarded member of the Clinical Faculty at U.C.L.A.'s Neuropsychiatric Institute.

Photo by Werner Amann.